THE GOULDIAN FINCH

THE
GOULDIAN FINCH

Stewart Evans and Mike Fidler

BLANDFORD PRESS
POOLE · NEW YORK · SYDNEY

First published in the UK 1986 by Blandford Press,
Link House, West Street, Poole, Dorset, BH15 1LL

Distributed in the United States by
Sterling Publishing Co., Inc.,
2 Park Avenue, New York, N.Y. 10016

Distributed in Australia by
Capricorn Link (Australia) Pty Ltd,
PO Box 665, Lane Cove, NSW 2066

British Library Cataloguing in Publication Data

Evans, Stewart
  The gouldian finch.
  1. Gouldian finch
  I. Title II. Fidler, Mike
  598.8'83   QL696.P244

ISBN 0 7137 1595 2

Typeset by Poole Typesetting (Wessex) Ltd.
Printed in Great Britain by Biddles Ltd., Guildford

CONTENTS

The striking, almost breath-taking, beauty of the Gouldian Finch has made it a firm favourite with aviculturists. It is now bred in Europe, the USA, Japan, South Africa, Australia and many other countries of the world, and has also been adopted as the emblem of several avicultural societies. At one time, however, it was regarded as a difficult and challenging species, which was hard enough to keep alive in captivity, let alone breed successfully. Fortunately, those days are largely behind us and, although the Gouldian Finch is still not a beginners' bird, any reasonably competent aviculturist should be able to cater for its needs. Paradoxically, its development as a cage bird is mirrored by a dramatic decline in its numbers in the wild. Wildlife authorities are concerned that this finch, which was once abundant across most of northern Australia, has become uncommon, or even rare, over large parts of its range.

There is therefore an urgent need for further research on this species and one of our objectives in writing this book is the hope that we may stimulate it. Field work is needed to determine the causes of the decline in wild birds, while aviculturists must continue to develop methods for its culture so that, come what may, its survival as a cage bird is guaranteed. We have set about our task with three additional aims. First, we have attempted to bring together published information on the Gouldian Finch, from articles which are scattered throughout a daunting number of magazines, books and learned scientific journals, so that it is available within a single cover. Second, we have given a detailed account of the culture of Gouldian Finches in captivity, based primarily on the practical experience and techniques developed by one of us, Mike Fidler, over a period of more than twenty years. In doing so, we have emphasised the importance of creating conditions in captivity which simulate the feeding and breeding conditions experienced by birds in the wild. Third, we have raised a number of controversial issues, such as the dangers of using Bengalese Finches as foster parents for Gouldian Finches and the need to set 'standards' to which all breeders should aim, with the deliberate intention of provoking thought and debate.

We would like to express our thanks to the numerous aviculturists and ornithologists who have helped us in various ways in preparing this book. Special mention must however be made to 21 breeders of Gouldian Finches in the UK who responded to a questionnaire about their stock and breeding methods; Ray Murray, who drew our attention to articles describing not only his own research but that of other Australian aviculturists; Mike Newman for advice on the chapter on exhibiting birds and for drawing Figure 15; Mike Coates for his bird drawings; Dennis Avon for his photographic work; Pat Joice for reading and checking the text; Margaret Munro for typing the bulk of the manuscript; and Liz Kinghorn for typing parts of it.

STEWART M. EVANS

MIKE E. FIDLER

March, 1985

Picture Credits

The publishers would like to thank the following for permission to reproduce illustrations.

Colour

Dennis Avon: Plates 1, 2, 3, 7, 12 and cover.
Stewart Evans: Plates 4 and 5.
D. L. Wright: Plates 6 and 10.
Ray Murray: Plate 8.
H.J. de Vos-Cayennedrees: Plate 11.
W.H. Keijzer: Plate 9.

Line Drawings

M. Coates: Figs. 5, 7, 8, 9, 10, 11, 12, 17 and 22.
Mike Newman: Fig. 15.
Stewart Evans: Figs. 1, 2, 3, 4, 6, 13, 14, 16, 18, 19, 20, 21, 23, 24 and 25.

Sources of information are indicated in the captions to Figures.

1 GOULD'S FINCH

The Gouldian Finch belongs to the family of birds known as the Estrildidae, which includes among others the waxbills, mannikins, parrot finches and grassfinches. They are all small seed-eating finches which are distributed over most of Africa, Asia and Australia. The charm and beauty of these feathered atoms, as they have been described, has always attracted the attention of aviculturists and they are among the most popular cage birds. Indeed, rather like parrots and pheasants, most species are far better known in captivity than in the wild. The reasons for their popularity are not hard to find. Many of them are relatively inexpensive to buy, are easily catered for in captivity and can be bred in small cages.

There are 19 members of the family which inhabit Australia, and the Gouldian Finch is the most strikingly-coloured of them. It was first described, and therefore known to science, as a result of an ornithological expedition to that part of the world which set out from England in May 1838 and was led by the zoologist John Gould. Gould himself returned three years later but left his assistant, John Gilbert, to explore the western part of the Australian continent. He obtained a specimen of the Gouldian Finch and sent it back to Gould, who described it and named it *Amandina gouldiae* (the generic name *Amandina* has since been changed: see below). Its specific name, *gouldiae*, which literally means belonging to Gould, was devoted to the memory of his wife Elizabeth, a brilliant illustrator of bird books, who had died after the expedition to Australia. He wrote:

It was with feelings of the purest affection that I ventured to dedicate this lovely bird to the memory of my late wife, who for many years laboriously assisted me with her pencil, accompanied me to Australia, and cheerfully interested herself in all my pursuits.

Gould's texts *Birds of Australia* are now standard reference books. They amount to 36 volumes which do full justice to his painstaking work.

DESCRIPTION

The Gouldian Finch almost defies description, with its vivid yellow, purple, green, blue, black, red and white areas of colouration, each distinctively separated from the others. To many aviculturists, it is the most beautiful of all birds. Others argue that its intense colours are overdone, and the claim has even been made that the title 'punk rocker of the bird world' is an appropriate one for it. There is, nevertheless, full agreement that it is one of the most fascinating of all species. It is certainly unique among the Estrildidae, if only for its extraordinary colouration.

The Adult Black-headed Male (Plate 1)

The general body colour, including the back and wings, is grass green; the tips of the wings are brown. The rump is cobalt blue and the tail feathers are black. There is a purple breast patch; the belly is yellow and the vent is white. The head and upper throat are black, and are encircled by a band of bright turquoise. The beak is pearly-white in colour but is tipped with red (or occasionally yellow; see Chapter 10). The feet are yellow and the eyes are dark brown.

The Adult Black-headed Female

She is similar to the male, but her colours are duller and less intense. The beak is blackish.

Immature Birds (Plate 2)

Juveniles do not acquire the adult colouration until the first moult. Before it, they are dull greenish-grey birds. The back, wings and tail are greenish-olive and the head, cheeks and neck ashy-grey. The tips of the wings are blackish-brown and the under-surface ashy-brown. Legs and feet are light brown; the eyes brown. The upper mandible of the beak is blackish and the lower one is reddish-white.

COLOUR VARIETIES

Almost as if the Gouldian Finch was not content with its brilliant colouration, it has three naturally-occurring colour varieties. In addition to the black-headed variety, there is a red-headed form (Plate 3, right) in which the normally black parts of the head are scarlet red, and a so-called yellow-headed form in which these parts of the head are orange (Plate 3, left). In the last century, some ornithologists even believed that the three varieties should be regarded as separate species, naming them as follows:

The black-headed variety: *Poephila gouldiae*

The red-headed variety: *Poephila mirabilis*

The yellow-headed variety: *Poephila armitiana*

The three occur together in the wild, however, and will readily interbreed with one another, so that there is no doubt that they should really be regarded as varieties of the same species.

The black-headed variety is easily the most common under natural conditions. The results of field surveys and counts of skins of Gouldian Finches in museums suggest that, overall, the ratio of black-headed birds to red-headed ones is about 3:1 (Table 1). The yellow-headed variety is rare and is said to occur in no more than about one per five to ten thousand birds. It is probably over-represented in museum collections simply because collectors tend to keep unusual examples in preference to common ones. There may also

TABLE 1

The numbers of Gouldian Finches of different head colours in the wild. Sources of information are included in the table.

Source of information	*Black-headed*		*Red-headed*		*Yellow-headed*	
	males	*females*	*males*	*females*	*males*	*females*
A. Keast (*Emu*, 1985, Vol. 58, pp. 219–246)	38	35	30	10	0	0
Skins in Australian museums visited by S. M. Evans in 1982	44	32	25	12	2	1
Wild-trapped birds imported to Newcastle University in 1983	8	11	2	1	0	0
S. M. Evans et al. (*Ibis*, 1985, Vol. 127, pp. 348–354)	49	42	13	7	0	0
Totals	139	120	70	30	2	1
Percentages	38.4	33.1	19.3	8.3	0.6	0.3

be minor differences in the colouration of Gouldian Finches from different geographic locations. There are reports that specimens from Napier and Broome in Western Australia have more brightly coloured heads, and backs of deeper shades of green, than those from Normanton in the eastern part of the country. Conversely, eastern birds are said to have more richly coloured under-parts of the body (Dr A. Keast: *Emu*, 1958, Vol. 58, pp. 219–246).

PRODUCTION OF COLOURS

Colouration of the plumage in the Gouldian Finch, and in other birds, is achieved in basically two ways. First, some colours are caused by coloured pigments in the feathers. Second, some colours (so-called structural colours) are the result of the optical properties of feathers: they produce coloured effects by the ways in which they reflect light.

It is surprising that, in spite of its extraordinary array of colours, the Gouldian Finch has only four pigments in its feathers. Two of these are known as *melanins: eumelanin* is a black pigment, and *phaeomelanin* is reddish-brown. The two remaining pigments belong to a group called carotenoids. One of them, the yellow pigment *lutein* is not actually manufactured in the bird's body but is absorbed from its food. The other is a red pigment, *astaxantin,* which is manufactured from lutein. The colours of some areas of plumage are due to the presence of a single pigment. The yellow of the belly region is, for example, the result of lutein in the features of that part of the body. Similarly, black-headedness is caused by eumelanin in the head feathers, red-headedness by astaxantin, and yellow-headedness by lutein (but see also Chapter 11). Dr A. M. Brush and Dr H. Seifried *(The Auk,* 1968, Vol. 85, pp. 416–430) showed that there are also differences in the structure of the head feathers in these varieties. The projections which make up the vanes of the head feathers (the barbs) are much finer in the black-headed birds than in the red and yellow-headed ones. The barbs which contain pigment in these latter two varieties are distinctively flattened (Fig. 1).

The Gouldian Finch, in common with most birds, does not manufacture a blue pigment. The blue regions of colouration, such as the rump patch and the head band, are the result of structural colours. The barbs of the feathers in these parts of the body are specially modified, and when they are viewed under the microscope it can be seen that they contain ranks of large thick-walled 'box' cells. These cells, together with a layer of melanin which is also present in the barbs, absorb any light that reaches them in the red end of the

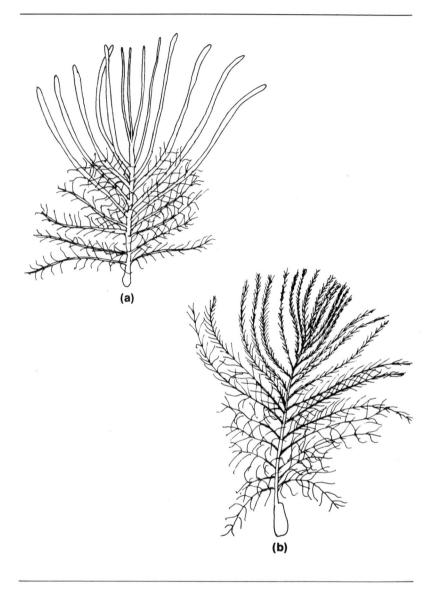

(a)

(b)

Fig. 1 *Differences in the structure of head feathers from two of the different head colour varieties of the Gouldian Finch. (a) A feather from a yellow-headed male; the main concentration of pigment is in the flattened, oar-shaped barbs. (b) A feather from a black-headed male; the pigment is contained in much finer barbs. The actual length of these feathers is about 3mm.*

spectrum but reflect that in the blue end. As a consequence, they appear blue.

Some colours are produced as the result of the combined effects of coloured pigments and structural colours. The feathers in the breast patch, for instance, produce structural blue but also possess the reddish-brown phaeomelanin. The latter modifies the blue effect, producing purple. Similarly, the green of the back and wings is a combined effect of structural blue and yellow lutein.

White areas of plumage are those in which no pigments are formed.

NOMENCLATURE

Biologists name organisms in order to avoid the confusions that can be caused by the use of common names. The Gouldian Finch, for instance, has also been (or is) known as the Lady Gould Finch, the Rainbow Finch and the Painted Finch. All of these names may seem appropriate but confusion arises when, for example, the species *Emblema picta* is also known as the Painted Finch.

Each species is given two names and, as we have already seen, the second (specific) of these *(gouldiae* in the case of the Gouldian Finch) is normally given by the person who describes it. The first (generic) name indicates relationships with other species, however, because closely-related species are grouped together in the same genus. Thus, the Longtail Finch, the Bicheno Finch, Parsons Finch and the Masked Finch are believed to be close relatives and all belong to the genus *Poephila*. They are named: *Poephila acuticauda, P. bichenovii, P. cincta* and *P. personata* respectively.

Stated in this way, the situation is simple enough, but problems arise when there is disagreement about relationships between species. This is the case in the Gouldian Finch. Gould himself thought that it was related to the Cut-throat Finch and some other African species and included it therefore in the genus *Amandina*. Any resemblences are, however, superficial and this view is no longer held. The current debate is whether it is really a grassfinch and should belong to the genus *Poephila*, a parrot finch *(Erythrura),* a mannikin *(Lonchura),* or should be included in a separate genus of its own, *Chloebia*. Arguments in favour of these alternatives are as follows.

1) The grassfinches *Poephila*. Dr Jean Delacour *(Zoologica,* 1943, Vol. 28, pp. 69–86) followed the example of earlier ornithologists by including it in the genus *Poephila* (see p. 9). He argued that Gouldian Finches resembled the grassfinches because of their bold plumage patterns. Furthermore, they have,

in common with them, attenuated tail feathers, and wings and beaks of similar shapes.

2) The parrot finches *Erythrura*. Mr I. G. Mitchell *(Emu,* 1958, Vol. 58, pp. 395–411) drew attention to four similarities in colouration between the Gouldian Finch and parrot finches. First, the pattern of head colours in the red-headed Gouldian Finch is similar to that in Peale's Parrot Finch. Second, the belly and breast colouration of the Gouldian Finch is like that of the Pin-tailed Nonpareil. Third, the colours of females of both the Gouldian Finch and parrot finches are similar to those of males but less intense. Fourth, the young of both are green or greyish-green birds.

The most convincing evidence that the Gouldian Finch is really a parrot finch comes from Mr Mitchell's comparisons of the mouth markings of young birds. The nestlings have strikingly-coloured and patterned mouths which probably help the parents to locate them in the darkness of the nest (see Chapter 3). The general pattern of markings of the young Gouldian Finch is very similar to that of the Red-headed Parrot Finch, particularly with regard to the development of two iridescent bluish-pearly nodules on the outside angle of the gaping mouth (Fig. 2). These nodules are absent in young grassfinches, and the pattern of markings inside the mouth is also different.

3) The mannikins *Lonchura*. Mrs M. F. Hall *(Symposium for the Zoological Society of London,* 1962, Vol. 8, pp. 37–70) found that the complex song of the male Gouldian Finch (it is described in Chapter 3) is similar to that of the mannikins. She also points out that the plumage pattern of the Gouldian Finch, although not the actual colours, is like that of the Chestnut-breasted Mannikin.

4) The genus *Chloebia*. Professor Klaus Immelmann *(Australian Finches in Bush and Aviary,* 1965, Angus and Robertson, Sydney) and Mr Derek Goodwin *(Estrildid Finches of the World,* 1982, British Museum and Oxford University Press) both argue that the Gouldian Finch is intermediate between the parrot finches and the mannikins and is therefore related to both of them. It may in fact represent an evolutionary link between the two genera. They

Fig. 2 *The markings inside the mouths of nestlings of three finches. The pattern of markings in the Gouldian Finch is similar to that of the Parrot Finch but unlike that of the Masked Grassfinch. (Based on a drawing by I. G. Mitchell. 1958. Emu. Vol. 58. pp 395-411).*

Gouldian Finch

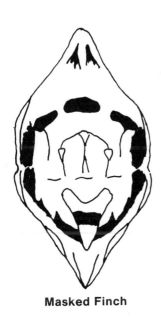

Masked Finch

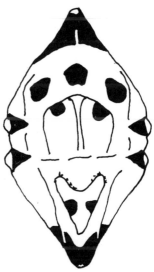

Red-headed Parrot Finch

15

suggest that the most satisfactory solution is to include it in the separate genus *Chloebia,* of which it is the only species.

This latter point of view is probably the most widely accepted and most authorities now describe it as *Chloebia gouldiae.*

2   NORTHERN AUSTRALIA: THE NATURAL HABITAT

There must have been many visitors to Australia who have looked forward to the opportunity of seeing the Gouldian Finch in its wild state. Most of them will have been disappointed. It inhabits northern parts of this vast land mass, well away from the southern and eastern centres of population, such as those of Perth, Adelaide, Melbourne, Sydney, Canberra and Brisbane. Travel is always difficult in the remote northern parts, except between major townships, and it becomes impossible off the beaten track for part of the year when the rains reduce the landscape to a quagmire. Indeed, it is a sobering thought that there are few Australian aviculturists, and even professional ornithologists, who have actually seen this species in its wild haunts.

DISTRIBUTION

The range of the Gouldian Finch is usually described as one which extends in a belt across northern Australia from the Kimberley in Western Australia, through Northern Territory and into the base of the Cape York Peninsula in northern Queensland (Fig. 3). The most recent information on its distribution is that provided by a survey carried out by members of the Royal Australasian Ornithological Union of all bird species. They recorded sightings of birds on the Australian continent with appropriate grid references. Subsequently, the vast amount of information was collated and plotted as a series of atlases. That for the Gouldian Finch shows that it still occurs throughout most of the range normally attributed to it, although it is almost certainly in smaller numbers than formerly (see Chapter 4).

It is generally believed, however, that the Gouldian Finch is nomadic in its habits. It does not breed in the more northerly part of its range, migrating southward before breeding (i.e. in the wet season). The return northward migration follows the breeding season.

CLIMATE

Northern Australia is subtropical and is therefore subject to high temperatures in the middle part of the day, commonly within the range of 30–45°C (86–113°F). It is also influenced by the monsoons which determine

(a)

(b)

Fig. 3 *The distribution of the Gouldian Finch in northern Australia. (a) The normally accepted distribution indicated by stipple (see e.g. D. Goodwin,* Estrildid Finches of the World, *1982, British Museum [Natural History] and Oxford University Press). (b) The distribution based on the recent RAOU survey. Symbols are used as follows:* ○ *recorded by less than 11 per cent of observers;* ○ *recorded by 11–40 per cent of them;* ○ *recorded by more than 40 per cent of them;* ● *recorded breeding by more than 40 per cent of them. (Redrawn from* The Atlas of Australian Birds *by M. Blakers, S.J.J.F. Davies and P.N. Reilly, 1984, Melbourne University Press.)*

the climate over the Indian Ocean and adjacent land masses. There are therefore two contrasting seasons: the wet season, which lasts from November until March, and the dry season, which extends over the remaining part of the year, from April until October.

The start of the wet season is marked by increased cloud cover and high humidity so that the air becomes sticky and oppressive. The rains are often torrential and, in extreme cases, as much as 50 cm (20 in) of water has been deposited within 24 hours. There is an enormous run-off of water from the land at these times and previously dry river-beds become raging torrents. Huge areas of land become flooded so that even main roads become impassable in places. The rain causes a dramatic change in the vegetation. The whole area springs to life as seeds which have lain dry and dormant for months germinate and grow rapidly in the wet, warm soil. There is also an explosion of animal life. Insects, including mosquitos and flying termites, become abundant, and frogs, toads and snakes come out of their dry season refuges. This is a time of abundant food for birds and the one during which most of them breed.

The dry season is characterised by clear blue skies, low humidities and almost no rain at all. Surface water becomes more and more scarce as the season progresses, and eventually becomes confined to major rivers, springs and waterholes (Plate 4). The soil becomes caked and dusty, and the formerly luxuriant vegetation becomes dry and parched. Many deep-rooted trees retain their green leaves but grasses and other surface-rooting plants dry up.

FLORA AND FAUNA

Much of northern Australia is covered by woodland, although this is often of a relatively open type, with widely-spaced trees and well-developed ground cover (Plate 5). In some parts, the trees give way to open grassland. Gum trees *(Eucalyptus)* are characteristic of much of the woodland. These beautiful trees are mostly confined to Australia in their natural state but there are about 400 different species distributed over the continent. Two important gums in northern woodlands are the bloodwood *Eucalyptus mophloia* and the white gum *Eucalyptus alba*. Sometimes there is an understorey of low shrubs, and here the she-oak *Casuaria* and the thorn *Acacia* are common. Ground cover is dominated by grasses of several different kinds but the hummock grass, or spinnifex, which forms mounds of up to a metre (3 ft) in height, is common in large areas.

Animal life is not always conspicuous, particularly in the hotter parts of the day, but it is nevertheless rich and abundant. Pouched mammals (the marsupials), including kangaroos and wallabies, frequent these parts. So too do reptiles: large monitor lizards, such as the goanna, are encountered, whereas Johnston's crocodile occurs in fresh-water pools, with its larger and more dangerous relative, the salt-water crocodile, in the brackish-water regions of rivers. This part of the world also includes a most impressive list of poisonous snakes. Bird life is almost unsurpassable. It ranges from the enormous emus and bustards to a variety of beautifully-coloured, but often excessively noisy, parrots: budgerigars, galahs and cockatoos are all common. Tiny birds are equally impressive, although they are usually more subtle and retiring in their habits, and less easily seen. They include some exotic wrens and many finches. In addition to the Gouldian Finch, the Bicheno (Doublebar) Finch, the Chestnut-breasted Mannikin, the Crimson Finch, the Longtail Finch, the Masked Finch, Parsons Finch, the Pictorella Mannikin, the Yellow-rumped Mannikin and the Zebra Finch are all inhabitants of these parts.

MAN AND THE ENVIRONMENT

The original inhabitants of these lands, the aborigines, lived in close harmony with the environment for generations and, until the settlement of Europeans, there was probably little change in the landscape. Two centuries of European colonisation have, unfortunately, left their mark and, although northern Australia is still characterised by its emptiness and largely unspoilt beauty, the signs of change are all too evident. The economic necessity of coaxing the land to yield its mineral wealth has seen the development of large mining enterprises. North-west Australia, for example, contains one of the largest iron ore deposits in the world and, since 1960, large international companies have banded together to exploit it. This is also diamond country and recent discoveries of rich seams have led to the rapid development of a new industry.

Agriculturally the land is rich but suffers from the prolonged dry season when growing conditions are poor. It is nevertheless suited to cattle farming, with ranches operating on a grandiose scale. They vary in size from a few hundreds to tens of thousands of square kilometres, and may support from less than a hundred to one hundred thousand head of cattle. Unfortunately over-grazing and trampling of the land by cattle, and possibly also the practice of burning large areas of grass during the dry season in order to encourage new growth the following wet, have already resulted in changes in the vegetation, posing potentially serious problems for the future of both farming and the natural fauna of the area. An attempt to counter the difficulties caused by the lack of water in the dry season has led to the Ord River Irrigation Scheme. This river has been dammed, creating the largest man-made lake in Australia. It stores nine times as much water as that contained in Sydney harbour, and this is used to irrigate farm land, in which crops of tropical fruits and vegetables are grown.

Unfortunately, the European settlers' habit of bringing animals from their home countries to Australia, sometimes deliberately, sometimes accidentally, has caused problems for other wildlife in the area. Many of the domestic animals have escaped and established wild (feral) populations which compete with the natural fauna. Other species have been introduced into the wild. Although the introduction of the rabbit is perhaps the extreme example, there are also well-established feral populations of dogs (dingos), cats, donkeys, water buffalo (introduced from Asia) and horses.

BIRD TRAPPING AND DECLINING NUMBERS OF THE GOULDIAN FINCH

The Gouldian Finch seems to be one of the casualties of man's colonisation of northern Australia. Dr Richard Zann has pointed out in the Royal Australasian Ornithologists' Union Newsletter (reprinted in *Australian Aviculture*, October 1984, p. 229) that there has been a serious decline in the numbers of this species over the past twenty years. A fall in numbers in Queensland has evidently been slow and consistent since the turn of the century but the decrease in numbers in the Northern Territory and the Kimberley has been sudden and dramatic. Ornithologists residing in Katherine (in Northern Territory) have, for example, seen the numbers drop from 'thousands' in the early 1960s, to 'hundreds' in the early 1970s, to a 'mere handful' in the 1980s.

It is difficult to single out a particular reason for the decline but it is probably related to some aspect of change in the habitat. There is also some concern that bird trapping for the cage bird market is, or may have been, a contributory factor. At one time, this was a thriving industry involving the export of thousands of finches but it was one which had undesirable aspects. Professor Immelmann (quoted in the English translation of G. Zeigler's book *The Gouldian Finch*, published by H. E. Iles Ltd) wrote of it as follows:

In 1958 alone, fifty-five professional catchers in the Kimberley caught 27,000 finches. They died in hundreds during the week long transportation in railway waggons through deserts to the nearest port, waiting there in overheated, underventilated sheds for the sailing of the next boat to take them to the towns of southern Australia. Many more died during air and sea transportation and in the hands of dealers. In the end no more than 300 to 400 of them could have survived.

Trappers use clap traps, which consist of two hinged and sprung metal frames covered with cord netting. They set them on the ground at waterholes, where finches aggregate in enormous numbers to drink during the dry season (see Chapter 3), in such a way that the birds must walk over them in order to reach the water. The spring mechanism is released, bringing the two halves together and trapping the birds inside.

Trapping has, however, been limited since the early 1960s as a result of the

TABLE 2

The numbers of finches trapped by licensed trappers between 1968 and 1982. The information is based on statistics published by the Western Australia Department of Fisheries and Wildlife. The summed totals only are shown for

Year	Gouldian Finch	Chestnut-breasted Finch	Pictorella Mannikin	Crimson Finch
1968	2078	56	1054	44
1969	1671	160	772	91
1970	1035	0	300	64
1971	3707	66	2590	822
1972	6498	8	1318	346
1973	6498	8	1318	346
1974	4558	458	3917	214
1975	4191	1059	791	299
1976	3775	428	986	186
1977	4573	3164	951	382
1978	1888	777	632	707
1979	1139	559	1723	579
1980	1128	1461	1956	1117
1981	1054	1179	1637	1735
1982	—	4243	1721	2250

Australian Government's (Prohibited Exports) Regulations which put a ban on the export of wildlife. The policy, which has been enforced by successive Governments, has stopped the trade in finches with foreign countries and thereby reduced the demand for them. Permits for the export of Australian native flora and fauna are now granted only occasionally and for genuine zoological or scientific purposes. Some finch trapping continues nevertheless in Western Australia, although this is the only state in which it is permitted. It is strictly under licence and is confined to a close season lasting from September 1 until November 15. The activity is centred on the town of Wyndham on the eastern edge of the Kimberley. Trapped birds, which are all sold within Australia, are sent to Perth and some of them go from there to other Australian cities. Trapping is a dying trade, however, since the Western Australia Department of Fisheries and Wildlife issues licences only to

the two years 1972 and 1973; they have been divided by two here and presented for each year separately. Small numbers of Painted Finches, Zebra Finches and Yellow-rumped Finches were included in the totals but are not presented individually. The Gouldian Finch was not trapped in 1982.

Star Finch	Longtail Finch	Bicheno Finch	Masked Finch	Total
1177	3247	268	846	8872
1300	3056	411	682	8184
1901	1468	114	295	5597
4362	6729	338	1901	20589
2352	5505	448	2148	19939
2352	5505	448	2148	19939
4815	4588	1824	1664	22038
5021	3616	1030	1015	18632
4753	5831	1117	2358	19433
3581	9267	1709	2866	26525
1524	4850	1425	1787	13590
4000	5210	1316	2306	16832
3579	6757	2279	2792	21076
4107	8543	2786	2409	23450
4082	4916	3158	2812	23214

existing trappers, and not to new applicants. According to Immelmann, there were 55 trappers operating in the Kimberley in 1958, but only 15 licences were issued in 1979 and 9 in 1982.

Trappers provide annual returns of the numbers of finches caught and these give the clearest evidence of the decline of the Gouldian Finch. They are summarised in Table 2. The total numbers of finches caught have fluctuated from year to year without any evidence of a decline in most species. In fact, the numbers trapped of several of them, including the Bicheno Finch, the Crimson Finch and the Chestnut-breasted Finch, have actually increased during the period surveyed. The Gouldian Finch shows a quite different trend. Numbers trapped have fallen dramatically from well over three thousand birds in most of the years from 1971 to 1977 to only just over a thousand by 1981. The decline is more evident when the numbers of Gouldian Finches trapped are considered as a percentage of all finches

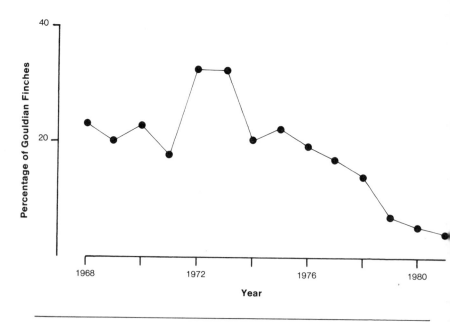

Fig. 4 *Decline in numbers of wild Gouldian Finches based on the numbers of birds caught by trappers in the Kimberley. Numbers of Gouldian Finches are expressed as a percentage of all finches caught. (Based on figures published by the Western Australia Department of Fisheries and Wildlife.)*

caught. As Fig. 4 shows, the decrease is from about 20 to 25 per cent in the early seventies to roughly 5 per cent in 1981. The Western Australia wildlife authorities decided, on the basis of these figures, to prohibit further trapping of the Gouldian Finch. Although it is unlikely that trapping itself is the major cause of the decline, it seems wise to prevent further pressure on an already threatened species. It is hoped that numbers will increase again but there is certainly no room for complacency.

As Dr Zann has pointed out, studies are urgently needed to determine the real cause of the fall in numbers, before it is too late to do something about it.

ILLEGAL TRAPPING AND BIRD SMUGGLING

One of the unfortunate effects of the strict export/import regulations is to increase the rarity, and therefore desirability and value, of some species to aviculture. This encourages illegal trapping and smuggling. There is unfortunately no doubt that this is occurring to some rare Australian parrots which are finding their way on to international markets. The World Wildlife Fund Australia Conservation Programme's booklet *Extinction is Forever* quotes a case of one of them, the Golden-shouldered Parrot:

In South Australia recently, the approach of a Government patrol caused bird smugglers to abandon their consignment of 198 illegally trapped parrots. The birds, cramped into seven boxes, were left in a creek bed and when found were all dead.

This is typical of the bird smuggling situation of the last decade or so in Australia. With our huge array of colourful indigenous species and restrictions placed on their export, the situation will continue to worsen. Unless something is done now.

A single Golden-shouldered Parrot is probably more valuable to a smuggler than a whole consignment of finches, and yet there is little doubt that some of these birds have been smuggled out of Australia. Species such as the Painted Finch, Pictorella Mannikin and the Red-browed Finch were unobtainable in Europe for many years but suddenly reappeared. It is widely believed that they were wild-trapped birds which had been shipped through bird markets in the Far East. Evidence of this kind undoubtedly gives aviculture a bad reputation, lending weight to the view, held by some conservationists, that it is undesirable since it provides the market for illegal trafficking in rare species. This is particularly unfortunate since the hobby, when properly managed, can make a real contribution to conservation by breeding threatened species in captivity.

3 LIFE UNDER NATURAL CONDITIONS

Animals must be adapted to cope with the demands placed on them within their particular habitats, whether these are in tropical, temperate or polar regions of the world. They must, for example, be able to tolerate the normal ranges of temperatures experienced in them, find food and shelter, breed successfully and escape from predators. As we have seen in the previous chapter, the Gouldian Finch lives in sub-tropical, arid regions of Australia, where there are dramatic seasonal changes in food and water supply. In this chapter, we shall consider the behaviour and habits of this species in the wild and, wherever appropriate, how these enable it to solve the problems of living in its demanding habitat.

The information presented here is based largely on observations by Professor Klaus Immelmann *(Australian Finches in Bush and Aviary*, 1965, Angus and Robertson, Sydney and London; and *Zoologische Jahrbücher Systematik Ökologie und Geographie der Tiere*, 1962, Vol. 90, pp. 1–196). The latter, more detailed, reference is in German.

FINDING FOOD

The Gouldian Finch exploits the different foods that are available at different times of the year. Grass seeds are abundant during the dry season and they then form the major component of its diet. It feeds especially on seeds of the grasses *Sorghum plumosum, Eriachne obtusa* and *Eragrostris*. It is an agile climber and takes seeds from the grass pannicles (seed heads) themselves while perched on vertical stems, steadying the particular pannicle on which it is feeding underfoot.

The short, stout beak of the Gouldian Finch, like that of other finches, is adapted to this seed-eating diet. It is used to dehusk seeds, whereby the non-nutritious seed covering is broken from the kernel and discarded. There are basically two ways in which finches do this. The Goldfinch and Parrot Finches slice their seeds in the beak. Each seed is taken between sharp cutting edges of the beak and, as a result of pronounced backward and forward movements of the jaw, the husk is sliced open (Fig. 5). It is then ejected. Painted Finches and several other finches dehusk seeds by crushing them. The seed is positioned against a horny pad on the upper mandible of the beak and then upward pressure from the lower jaw crushes and breaks the husk.

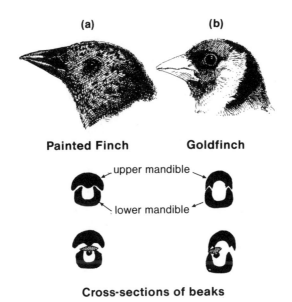

(a)   **(b)**

Painted Finch   Goldfinch

upper mandible

lower mandible

Cross-sections of beaks

Fig. 5 *The two methods employed by finches in dehusking seeds. (a) The Painted Finch's method of crushing them against a hard projection of the upper mandible (beak). The tongue, which pushes the seed into place is shown in the lower diagram of the cross-section of the beak. (b) The technique used by the Goldfinch, and also Parrot Finches, of slicing seeds on cutting edges on the margin of the beak.*

There have been no detailed studies of dehusking in the Gouldian Finch but the internal structure of its beak suggests that it may use the Parrot Finch's method of slicing seeds. Observations are needed to confirm this point.

Grass seeds germinate with the onset of rains in the wet season and are no longer available as food. The Gouldian Finch then switches its diet to exploit the new crop of ripening seeds. It also becomes insectivorous, feeding more on insects than any of the other Australian finches. It is a skilled hunter, taking flying termites on the wing, searching cobwebs for spiders and trapped insects, and taking beetles from the ground.

WATER REQUIREMENTS

Drought is a predictable event during the dry season in northern and central

Australia, where water in large areas of land becomes restricted to a few waterholes and springs. This substance comprises about 70 per cent of the bird's body, and must be kept at this high level for survival. It is, however, lost from the body as a result of two essential processes. First, the bird's droppings contain water. They must be moist in order to be voided and to carry the excretory products. Second, water is lost by evaporation through the skin and from the lungs and mouth in air which is breathed out. Evaporation is important, however, because it cools the body in much the same way as the evaporation of sweat cools our bodies. Evaporative cooling is vital in a hot climate, and the warmer the temperature the greater the loss of water from it. Overall, water losses can be severe. These processes have been studied in detail in the Zebra Finch, which, in spite of its small size (weighing perhaps 12–15g), may lose more than 2g of water per day in its droppings and a further 1g as a result of evaporative cooling (Table 3).

TABLE 3
The water budget of the Zebra Finch over a period of 24 hours.

Water gain (g)		
	Water in food eaten	2.03
	Metabolic water from food	0.46
	Total gain	2.49
Water loss (g)		
	Water lost in droppings	2.03
	Water lost by evaporation from body	1.23
	Total loss	3.46
Average daily water deficit		0.97

Water which is lost from the body must be replenished in some way, but drinking is not the only means by which this can be done. Food invariably contains some water and this can make up part of the deficit. The dry season diet of dry seeds in the Gouldian Finch is relatively poor in water (about 7–10 per cent) but the foods of some other birds are so rich in it that they can provide all of the water requirement. Some African finches, for instance, switch from a diet of dry seeds to one of insects, which have a high water content, at times of drought. By doing so, they can survive for months without drinking at all. The Zebra Finch, like the Gouldian Finch, remains on its seed diet during the dry season but it may nevertheless gain as much as 2g of water per day from it (Table 3). A second source of water, other than that gained by drinking, is so-called metabolic water. It is a by-product of the metabolic breakdown of stored fats and carbohydrates inside the bird's body. The Zebra Finch gains about 0.5g of water per day in this way.

Most birds still suffer a daily water deficit: the water lost in the droppings and by evaporative cooling is greater than that gained from the food itself and from the metabolism of food (Table 3). This deficit must be made good by drinking and consequently they make regular (at least daily) visits to watering places, often making characteristic and highly purposeful flights to them at predictable times of day; so much so that they have been used by travellers in the bush as indicators of water. Mr H. Lindsay writes in his notes under the heading 'Bushcraft – water-finding' in the *Australian Encyclopedia* (edited by A. M. Chisholme, published by Angus and Robertson, Sydney) as follows:

Various species of Australian Birds are infallible guides to water; they include wild pigeons, which always drink at sunset and whose hovering lines of flight indicate where the waterhole lies, several species of finch, various parrots, the mudlark or peewee, and the large brolga or native companion.

Dr S. J. J. F. Davies (1972, *Emu*, Vol. 72, pp. 8–12) documented the regular patterns of visits made by birds and some mammals to waterholes in desert regions of Western Australia. Crested Pigeons were early morning visitors, Emus and Zebra Finches drank in the middle part of the day, and Galahs came to the water in the late afternoon. Mammals, including the Red Kangaroo, tended to drink during the night.

A larger range of finches was recorded in studies of drinking behaviour in that part of north-west Australia known as the Kimberley (S. M. Evans, J. A. Collins, R. Evans, and S. Miller, 1985, *Ibis*, Vol. 127, pp. 348–353). Gouldian Finches usually drank in the early mornings, before 0700, arriving in groups at the water (Fig. 6). Members of groups normally spent about 10–20 minutes perched in trees adjacent to the water, evidently on the look-out for predators, before going down to drink. Eventually, individuals flew to the ground and drank in a series of long gulps. Only about a minute was spent on the ground. Birds reassembled in perching places, before flying off to foraging grounds, usually some distance away. Gouldian Finches only

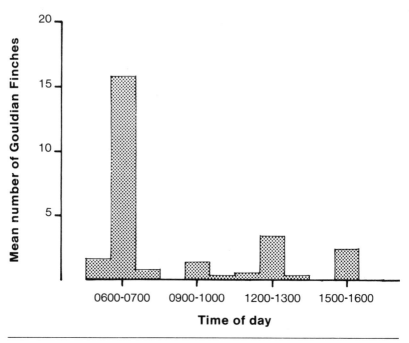

Fig. 6 *The arrival of Gouldian Finches at different times of day at waterholes during the dry season. The number of finches shown for each hour is the mean for information from 9 waterholes in the Kimberley. (Based on data in a paper by S.M. Evans, J.A. Collins, R. Evans and S. Miller, 1985,* Ibis, *Vol. 127, pp. 348–354).*

occasionally visited watering places in the late morning, afternoon or evening, and may therefore have taken water only once per day. Pictorella Mannikins had similar habits to Gouldian Finches, evidently drinking once per day in the early mornings. Bicheno Finches, Longtail Finches and Masked Finches were also early morning visitors to waterholes, but they foraged on nearby grasses, and returned to the water at frequent intervals during the morning and early afternoon. The habits of Star Finches were like those of Zebra Finches (see above); they mostly drank in the middle part of the day.

The Gouldian Finch drinks by sucking water (Fig. 7). This is unlike the method used by most other birds which swallow water; they dip the beak into the water, take some of it into the mouth and then lift the head in order to swallow it. The Gouldian Finch, however, keeps the beak continuously in contact with the water and fluid is sucked up by means of peristaltic

Fig. 7 *A Gouldian Finch drinking by the characteristic method of sucking up water.*

movements of the oesophagus. This method is also employed by African Desert Mouse Birds and other Australian finches which inhabit arid or semi-arid environments, including the Bicheno Finch, the Star Finch and the Zebra Finch. Presumably, drinking in this way is advantageous during drought conditions. One possibility is that is enables birds to suck up, and thereby exploit, the tiny quantities of water which are deposited overnight as dewdrops on vegetation. Another possibility is that individuals can imbibe water more rapidly by sucking than by swallowing and thereby spend less time at waterholes, where they are at high risk of attack from predators (see below).

COURTSHIP AND PAIR FORMATION

Breeding occurs in the latter part of the wet season and, as in other Australian and African finches, it is timed to coincide with the abundance of seeding grasses and insects which follows the rains. Paired Gouldian Finches remain together throughout the breeding season and co-operate with one another in rearing two or three broods in rapid succession. The bond between them remains intact for only one season, however, and is therefore less permanent than that in many other finches, which pair for life. Mated Gouldian Finches separate after breeding and then re-pair in the following season. It is also interesting that members of Gouldian Finch pairs are less attentive to one another than those of most related species. Pairs of Zebra Finches and grassfinches, for example, regularly perch in bodily contact and preen one another.

Male Gouldian Finches spend a lot of time singing as the breeding season approaches. The function of the song is not fully understood but it may be concerned with the attraction of potential mates. Certainly, in captivity, singing males attract an audience, although this may include other males and immature birds, as well as females. The listeners perch close to the singer and

Fig. 8 *The posture adopted by a bird which is peering (on the left). Sometimes the peering individual perches so close to the singing bird (on the right) that the latter is forced to lean away.*

adopt a characteristic posture known as peering (Fig. 8) in which they give every impression of listening intently to the song.

The actual process of pair formation involves a complicated and, to our eyes, comical ritual in which the male performs an elaborate dance in front of his intended spouse. This courtship performance normally takes place on a horizontal branch in the centre of a tall tree. During it, the male adopts postures in which he displays his gaudy colouration to the full. The ritual actually consists of two phases. In the first of these, the male perches obliquely (Fig. 9). The feathers of the face are partially fluffed and those on the back of the head are fully fluffed, exaggerating the colours of the head and framing them with the bright turquoise band which surrounds them. At the same time, the breast and belly feathers are fluffed so that the purple breast patch is enlarged. The tail is twisted towards the female displaying the blue rump

Fig. 9 *The oblique posture which is adopted by the male Gouldian Finch during the first phase of its courtship display.*

patch to her. Brilliant colouration alone is, however, insufficient to impress the female. If the male is to gain her affections, he must also display to her. He first makes a series of head movements (beak wipes) in which the beak is wiped to and fro across the perch (without normally touching it). The beak and head are now shaken extremely rapidly in front of the female. The mood suddenly changes and the second phase of the ritual commences. The bird now adopts an upright posture on the perch with the beak pointed downward (Fig. 10). He alternately stretches and flexes his legs so that he bobs up and down, usually making a series of 'on the spot' jumps, as he sings his courtship song. The whole performance may be repeated several times.

If the female is unimpressed by the male's display, she may simply fly away leaving him to search for another partner. The receptive female, however, remains near him and may respond by shaking her body plumage and twisting her tail in his direction. She may also make head movements which are similar to, but less intense and exaggerated, than those of the male.

Fig. 10 *The upright posture which is adopted by the male Gouldian Finch during the second phase of its courtship display. Note the 'twisted' tails of both the male and the female.*

NESTING

Once the birds have paired, nesting activities can commence. The Gouldian Finch is predominantly hole-nesting, choosing cavities in the trunks of tall trees, as well as the vacated nests of kingfishers and parrots in termite mounds. They are highly social in their nesting habits and several pairs may nest together in a large hollow. Nests may be lined with short pieces of grass or may lack them altogether; some pairs simply rearrange the debris within the hole as the nest. Other pairs (probably about 25 per cent of them) build nests in trees or bushes, commonly in the forks of major branches. These nests are made of grass stems but are poorly constructed. Some of them have a loosely-made roof; others lack it.

The male searches for the nest site, although he is extremely cautious in entering any newly discovered crevice or hole. Such places may already be occupied by other birds or, more seriously, by predatory snakes. Not surprisingly, his initial explorations are brief and nervous. Eventually, however, he is reassured and, if the site is suitable, he makes characteristic nest calls to his mate, enticing her to follow him into their new home. Collection of nest materials is by the male alone.

Copulation is believed to occur in the nest, although captive birds sometimes mate on perches or on the ground (see Chapter 9).

EGG-LAYING AND INCUBATION

Eggs are laid one per day, usually in the early mornings. They are white in colour and clutches of them vary in size from about 4 to 9 eggs. The beginning of incubation is a gradual process and parents may spend some time sitting in the nest without actually covering the eggs. Nevertheless, the process proper often starts before the last egg is laid. The result is that the embryos in some eggs may be more advanced in their development than those in others, and hatching may occur over a relatively long period of two or three days.

Incubation duties are shared during the daylight but the female performs them on her own at night. Their main function is to maintain the eggs at the correct temperature for their development. A bare area of skin, known as the brood patch, develops on the underside of both the male and female during the breeding season (Plate 6). It is brought into direct contact with the eggs during incubation. The skin here is generally flabby and this allows it to make close contact with the eggs by fitting round their contours. It is also rich in blood vessels, and this improves its efficiency as a heat exchanger.

Incubation is not necessarily continuous, however. The eggs can be left for periods of several hours without coming to any harm in the warm climate of the natural habitat. Indeed, Gouldian Finches regularly leave their clutches of eggs in order to join the daily social gatherings that occur during the breeding season (see below). Parents may also stop incubating their eggs when the outside temperatures exceed about 37°C (98.6°F), presumably because they become in danger of over-heating.

Nest relief, when one member of a pair takes over incubation duties from its partner, occurs inside the nest; the non-incubating bird enters the nest, making characteristic calls as it does so. Soon afterwards, its partner leaves.

REARING THE YOUNG

Incubation of the eggs lasts for about 14 to 15 days before the young hatch. Pieces of broken and discarded egg shell are devoured by the parents. The chicks are fed from the first day onward by both parents, on regurgitated food which is pumped into the gaping mouths of the young and, from there, into the crop. The chick's crop extends to both sides of the neck but, in the very young, only one side, that on the chick's right, is filled with food. Subsequently, both sides of the crop are filled. Chicks beg actively for food and compete intensely with one another for their parents' attention by making loud begging calls which can be heard several metres from the nest. The nestlings also possess conspicuous markings on the inside of the mouth and tongue, and luminous nodules on the base of the beak (see Fig. 2). These almost certainly help parents to locate the mouths of their young in the dim light of the nest. There are two begging postures. Newly-hatched nestlings lift the head and beak upward to an angle of about 45–60° from the body. Older ones (including those which have left the nest) keep the head low but twist the neck to one side, directing the mouth upward (Fig. 11).

Newly-hatched Gouldian Finches lack any covering of down and are of a light flesh colour. Their eyes open between the seventh and tenth days of life, and the tips of the first primary feathers break through the skin on the eleventh or twelfth day. Young fledge when they are about 21 or 22 days old, although they may remain in the nest for longer than this in some circumstances.

This is the case, for example, when prolonged rainfall restricts the foraging activities of the parents, and the consequent shortage of food retards the development of their young. Once young birds have left the nest they do not

Fig. 11 *A female Gouldian Finch feeding a fledgling.*

return to it (although captive birds sometimes roost there). They do nevertheless remain in its vicinity for several days, where they are fed by both parents. Young are undoubtedly recognised by their parents who feed them exclusively, even when they are in groups with other young birds.

Fledglings become independent at five weeks of age. Their sexual development is rapid, particularly in males, which may start to sing and court females soon after leaving the nest. Professor Immelmann reports that he had observed behaviour of these kinds in birds which are still being fed by their parents. Young from early broods may breed when they are no more than eight weeks old and can produce young in the same season as they themselves hatch.

THE MOULT

Breeding is an energy-demanding process and it is important that other processes, which drain the bird's resources, do not conflict with it. The moult is a particularly significant one since the bird, in shedding one set of feathers, must manufacture a completely new outfit (see Chapter 7). Adult birds avoid this potential conflict by moulting after breeding activities have ceased.

Juvenile birds may start to moult at the age of about six to eight weeks but the process is a slow one, taking several months. There is a sequence in which different parts of the juvenile's plumage are replaced, gradually revealing its adult colours. The feathers of the belly are the first to be renewed, followed by those on the rump patch. The head now begins to moult, as does the breast patch. The feathers of the back and wings are then replaced and, finally, the long central tail feathers make their appearance.

SOCIAL BEHAVIOUR

Gouldian finches normally occur in flocks during the dry season and these become larger, often forming groups of hundreds or even thousands of individuals, as water becomes more and more scarce. The flocks split up again with the first rains, and birds disperse over a wide area. Social activities continue during the breeding season, however, and members of a breeding colony regularly aggregate together, usually in the late afternoon. They make loud contact calls as they assemble and may then feed as a group, bathe together or just perch close to one another.

AVOIDING PREDATORS

Predators play significant roles in controlling populations of most animals. Professor Immelmann believes, however, that due to its bright colouration, and therefore conspicuousness, the Gouldian Finch may be subject to particularly high levels of predation. It is more prolific than most other

Fig. 12 *An Australian Goshawk. It is a natural predator of the Gouldian Finch and other small birds and often attacks them when they are drinking at waterholes.*

Australian finches, rearing as many as 15 to 20 young per pair in a season, and Immelmann suggests that this may be necessary simply to maintain populations at satisfactory levels.

The nesting period is one in which finches are highly susceptible to attack and snakes and small mammals probably take a heavy toll of eggs and young. The carnage undoubtedly continues beyond this stage, however, and adult Gouldian Finches are at particularly high risk when they visit waterholes to drink. Predators, such as the Australian Goshawk (Fig. 12), the Kookaburra, butcher birds and feral cats, visit these places and use them as ready sources of prey. It is not surprising therefore that finches are extremely cautious in going down to the water to drink (see above). They are equally nervous while drinking and periodically interrupt the act to look up and scan their surroundings for signs of danger. When attack does occur, drinking birds, together with those still waiting to drink, fly away from the area. There is therefore a dramatic change at the waterhole: the place which was formerly bustling with activity becomes quiet and deserted.

CALLS AND SONG

Vocalisations are an important means by which birds communicate with one another, and we have already referred to the courtship song and several of the calls of young and adult Gouldian Finches, without attempting to describe them. Traditionally, ornithologists have described calls verbally. For example, the two contact calls which are made by Gouldian Finches which have lost sight of their mates or other members of the social group have been described as 'ssit-ssit' and 'ssreeh'. Unfortunately, such descriptions are subjective and often difficult to interpret. A more objective method of analysing and describing calls is by use of the sound spectrograph, or sonagraph. This produces a visual picture of the sound (a sonagram) in which its frequency (in kilohertz) is plotted against time (in seconds). Figure 13 shows sonagrams of the two contact calls mentioned above. They are quite different from one another in structure. The 'ssit-ssit' call has a frequency range which extends from about 5 to 8 kilohertz but lasts for only about a tenth of a second. The 'ssreeh' call covers a much narrower frequency band between about 6 and 7 kilohertz and lasts for about half a second.

These calls are much simpler in structure than the Gouldian Finch's song, which is complex by any standards. Indeed, it is more complex than that in any of the other members of the Estrildidae (see Fig. 19). It is a high-pitched, soft, almost whispering rendition, which is inaudible to the human ear at more than a few metres. It consists of a long series of different elements and, as Fig. 14 illustrates, individual ones may not be repeated in a song lasting for several seconds.

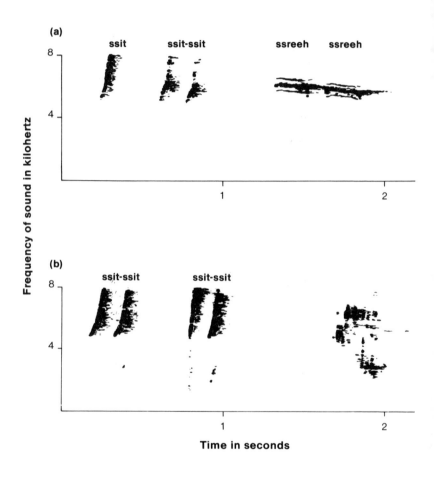

Fig. 13 *Sonagrams (sound spectrographs) of the contact calls of Gouldian Finches. (a) The 'ssit-ssit' and 'ssreeh' calls of wild-trapped birds; (b) the 'ssit-ssit' call and one abnormal call made by domestically-bred birds.*

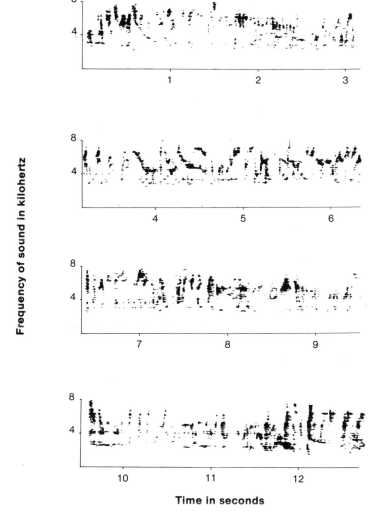

Fig. 14 *A sonagram (sound spectrograph) of a song of a Gouldian Finch lasting for more than 12 seconds. There is no repetition throughout this period.*

4 HISTORY OF THE GOULDIAN FINCH IN CAPTIVITY

The Gouldian Finch has been kept as a cage bird for roughly a hundred years. The first importation of live birds into Europe was evidently into Germany in 1886, and these birds are said to have bred during the following year. Dr E. P. Ramsay was successful in rearing them in aviaries at the Australian Museum in Sydney in 1888 and Queenslanders also claimed breeding successes at about this time. Mr Reginald Phillips bred Gouldian Finches in the United Kingdom in 1891. His birds nested in a dead tree trunk which had been fixed in their flight, weaving a grass nest which was domed and with an entrance at the top. Mr Phillips was also able to interbreed different head colour varieties, showing that they were of the same species. Many had believed that the black-headed bird was an immature red-head, whereas others thought that the three head colour varieties were different species (see also Chapter 1).

The Gouldian Finch was always regarded as a challenging species and, in the early days, many people had difficulty in keeping it alive, let alone breeding from it. The Englishman Mr P. W. Teague was probably the most successful of the early breeders. He started with two pairs of Gouldian Finches in 1926 and these formed the basis of a stud which continued through 30 unbroken years until 1956, when ill health forced him to give up his life's hobby. Herr Gert Zeigler is also well-known in Europe for his knowledge of, and success in keeping these birds, as are Mr E. Baxter and Mr Ray Murray in Australia, and Mr F. Barnicoat in South Africa. The writings of these and other aviculturists testify to the early difficulties and frustrations of keeping the Gouldian Finch. Teague wrote as follows in an article in the *Avicultural Magazine* (1932, Vol. 10, pp. 90–99):

I have specialized in these birds and I can claim to have been fairly successful with them, but beginning with Gouldian Finches in England was anything but a cheerful proposition, for practically the only information I could get was "Yes, very beautiful birds, but they only seem to die", or "they don't last long – like spring flowers". I enquired from as many sources as I could including members of the A.S., and these are a few of the encouraging replies I got. No. 1. "Once acclimatized they do quite well for a time, and most of them will attempt nesting, but my experience is, that the young very rarely live more than three to four months – I have had nest after nest of them and all have gone the same way, so I have given them up in despair." No. 2. "I commenced the season with four pairs and have now only one cock bird left – all seem to die for no apparent reason." No. 3. "They are very beautiful but not worth wasting money on, sell them out as soon as you can and cut your losses." I nearly did this, for all had the same cheerful tale. However, I decided to try methods which had proved very successful with birds I had kept when abroad, although many things I use now were unobtainable there.

There has been enormous progress in the culture of this species since Teague's first experiences with them, and nowadays any reasonably competent aviculturist should be capable of keeping them successfully. Nevertheless, a short poem, entitled *Ode to the Gouldian Finch*, which appeared in *Cage and Aviary Birds* (May 7, 1983) more than fifty years after Teague's article, suggests that all is neither forgotten nor forgiven:

A Gouldian man stood at the gate, his head bent very low.
He sadly asked the Man of Fate which way he had to go.
"What hast thou done?" St Peter asked, "To seek admission here?"
"I bred Gouldian Finches, Sir," he said, "For many and many a year".
"Bred Gouldian Finches?" St Peter cried, then gently pressed the bell.
"Step inside and choose your place, you've had your share of hell!"

THE PROBLEMS

One of the many problems confronting aviculturists was the difficulty in acclimatising stock which was newly-exported from Australia. Birds which survived the rigours of the journey were inevitably in poor condition and were often expected to cope with cold, damp climates in temperate regions of the world. Mr. H. R. Gilbert *(Australian Aviculture,* November 1959, pp. 159–164) sums up the problems of keeping them in England as follows:

I am convinced that practically all of the troubles attributed to the keeping of these birds are associated with the problem of getting them acclimatised. Freshly imported specimens are tricky subjects to acclimatise, and arriving in this country as most of them do during our winter months accentuates the problem.

The general recommendation was that newly-arrived birds should be kept at temperatures of not less than 15–20°C (59–68°F) which are still relatively low compared with those experienced in the natural habitat. Access to outdoor aviaries was not normally permitted until the birds had been acclimatised for several weeks and then they were only allowed to fly in well-protected flights. Once acclimatised, however, the Gouldian Finch can be remarkably hardy. Teague, for instance, kept his birds in unheated, but covered, aviaries throughout the year. Today, there are many European breeders who allow their birds access to outdoor flights, even when there is frost or snow on the ground. Almost all of them do, nevertheless, provide dry, draught-proof and heated quarters in which the birds can roost and escape from the most severe weather (see also Chapter 9).

Gouldian Finches, even newly-imported ones, were often eager to nest in captivity. They would do so either when kept in colonies in aviaries or when housed as separate pairs in small cages. Experiences in rearing young from them varied enormously, however. Some aviculturists claimed considerable success, whereas others, probably the large majority, reported failure after failure. Egg-binding in females was a common problem, as was the habit, probably due to the male, of throwing young out of the nest as soon as they hatched from the egg. The major frustration was, nevertheless, the high mortality that often occurred in fledged young during the first moult. Mr Ray Murray *(Australian Aviculture,* October 1953, pp. 116–121) lost 12 young out of 50 bred in 1951 (24 per cent) in this way, and 7 out of 56 (12.5 per cent) in 1952. Mr L. Koenig *(Australian Aviculture,* July 1953, p. 300) had even worse losses of about 75 per cent per annum. Similar problems were reported in Europe. Herr Gert Zeigler *(The Gouldian Finch,* translated from the German and published by H. E. Iles Ltd) describes the results of a survey of 30 breeders in Germany, Austria, Switzerland and Holland. Overall, they lost 148 out of 413 young birds (36 per cent) during the first moult, and about 33 per cent of those remaining in the next moult.

The cause of death was not immediately obvious, but Mr Ray Murray *(Australian Aviculture,* October 1953, p. 118) noticed that those birds which succumbed were poor specimens and described the symptoms as follows:

The disease or whatever it may be that causes so high a mortality amongst the youngsters certainly has us all baffled. With me, the trouble seems to appear when the youngsters start to moult. The drooping of its wing and the ruffling of its feathers is usually the first sign that something is wrong. It will tuck its head under its wing and stay like this on the perch for most of the day. In the advanced stage I have watched a bird fly down off the perch and appear as if it is searching for something that is not there in the seed tin or on the floor. It has picked up a seed, rolled it round its beak and dropped it without dehusking it.

Mr Brian Burgess *(Australian Aviculture,* January 1951, pp. 4–5; and

February 1951, pp. 19–20) believed that an inadequate diet was the basic problem, and attributed death to protein deficiency. He quotes examples of two breeders who had enormous successes when they gave their Gouldian Finches access to seeding grasses (which are relatively rich in proteins; see Chapter 7). Two pairs belonging to one of these breeders reared 65 young between them in a single season, including nests of 8 and 9 young. Teague's own successes also seem to have been related to the provision of an adequate and varied diet. He supplemented his birds' food with vitamin preparations, seeding grasses and soaked seeds, in addition to the following mixture of mineral salts:

Sterilised feeding bone flour:	1.1kg	(38 oz)
Carbonate of lime	1.3kg	(47 oz)
Salt	340g	(12 oz)
Sulphur	57g	(2 oz)
Ferric oxide	28g	(1 oz)
Potassium iodide	42g	(1.5 oz)

Nowadays, mortality during the first moult is not a serious problem, probably because the importance of providing an adequate diet is more generally understood. The moult is nevertheless still a time of strain on the bird's resources, and diet deficiencies are not the only possible causes of death during it. Mr Koenig believed that his heavy losses (see above) were due to inadequate housing conditions. He kept young birds in outside flights which were open to all weathers. Dramatically improved results were reported, however, with almost no losses at all, when he changed his flights to semi-enclosed ones, with covered roofs.

THE ROLE OF BENGALESE FINCHES AS FOSTER PARENTS

Until the 1960s, the export of large numbers of wild-trapped birds from Australia ensured that Gouldian Finches were available for sale throughout the world, irrespective of the success of aviculturists in breeding them in captivity. The Australian Government's ban on the export of wildlife, however, caused a sudden change in the situation. From that time onwards, the only birds for sale have been domestically-bred ones. This has presented a real challenge to aviculturists but one to which they reacted successfully. They have established not only the Gouldian Finch but most of the other

Australian finches in captivity. It is an impressive statistic that, more than 20 years after the ban, the numbers of different species which can be purchased in, for example, the United Kingdom and South Africa, is similar to that in Queensland and South Australia, where some wild-trapped birds are still available (see Chapter 2 and Table 4). The only differences in the lists are that the White-eared Masked Finch, the Beautiful Firetail and the Red-eared

TABLE 4
Finches available for sale in Australia (South Australia and Queensland), South Africa and the United Kingdom, and the approximate prices charged for them, during 1982/1983. Prices are quoted in £. * indicates that a species is not available; + indicates that it is available but no price is quoted. Information from the Avicultural Society of South Australia *Bird Price Guide* 1982–83 and *The Grassfinch* (April 1983, Vol. 7, p. 40).

| Species | Country/State and Price per Pair | | | |
	South Australia	Queensland	South Africa	United Kingdom
Gouldian Finch (normal)	16–19	18	13	35
Gouldian Finch (white-breasted)	*	*	43	60
Longtail Finch (including Heck's Finch)	7–11	15	14	30
Bicheno Finch	10	4–14	36	35
Parsons Finch	17	19–28	23	30
Star Finch (normal)	6	7	16	25
Star Finch (yellow-headed)	19	14	135	90
Cherry Finch	10	9	25	35
Painted Finch	9	22	320	150
Chestnut-breasted Finch	5	3	27	40
Blue-faced Parrot Finch	33	28	32	35
Red-eared Firetail	+	+	*	*
Beautiful Firetail	+	+	*	*
Pictorella Finch	10	19	135	120
Crimson Finch	16	20	135	150
Yellow-rumped Finch	10	14	160	90
Sydney Waxbill	8	6	160	150
Diamond Finch	17	20	36	40
Masked Finch	9	17	50	50
White-eared Masked Finch	+	55	*	*

Firetail are available in Australia, but they are relatively uncommon even in aviaries there.

This success story was not due simply to improved methods of keeping Australian finches. Breeders relied heavily on the use of Bengalese Finches as foster parents. The technique is described in more detail in Chapter 10, but basically clutches of eggs laid by Gouldian (or other) Finches are placed under pairs of Bengalese Finches, which incubate them and then rear the nestlings. Even Teague used this method to some extent. He recommended that all breeders of foreign finches should keep a few of these 'wonderful little foster parents' and comments that pairs of Bengalese will sometimes incubate and rear young when they themselves have not laid eggs.

The technique of fostering-rearing was older than this, however, and had previously been used on a commercial scale in Japan. According to Dr Jean Delacour *(Avicultural Magazine,* August 1926, p. 213) bird breeding enterprises were concentrated mainly in the Tuner Sea area and in and around the city of Osaka. Each breeding establishment had several hundreds of box cages, roughly 60 × 60 × 60 cm (2 × 2 × 2 ft) in dimension, arranged in four or five rows, one on top of another. There was one pair of birds per cage, in which grass and coconut fibre was provided as nesting material. Most breeders had fifty or so pairs of canaries and Java Sparrows, and about the same numbers of Australian finches. Whereas the canaries and Java Sparrows reared their own young, there were some 200 pairs of Bengalese Finches acting as foster parents for the Australian finches. Many thousands of them were reared in this way and large numbers were exported to Europe and elsewhere. Evidently, however, the quality of the birds suffered because the breeders were attempting to produce them in too large quantities. The export trade declined and is now negligible, if it exists at all.

The practice of foster-rearing has not, however, ceased and it is still carried out on a commercial scale in Holland, Belgium and the USA. One large establishment, *Behavioral Studies of Birds,* for example, rears both Gouldian Finches and Bicheno Finches by this method. According to Renata Decher-Juden *(Cage and Aviary Birds,* May 21, 1983, p. 1) eggs laid by some 500 pairs of finches are hatched and reared by about 2000 pairs of Bengalese Finches. Clutch after clutch of eggs is taken from pairs of Gouldian Finches over a breeding season which lasts for nine months, and it is claimed that as many as 60 eggs can be taken from a single female without putting undue strain on her. We feel that this procedure is excessively over-demanding and do not recommend it, although only time will tell whether the birds will decline in quality as a result of it. An interesting argument is presented in favour of the foster-rearing method by this author. It is claimed that it can be used to break parasite life cycles. Parents infect their young with their own parasites but Bengalese Finches do not harbour many of the normal Gouldian Finch parasites and cannot therefore transmit them to the young under their care.

Commercial breeding on this scale does not occur in the United Kingdom

TABLE 5

The results of a survey of Gouldian Finch breeders in the United Kingdom. It shows the total numbers of young reared by 20 of them in 1983, and the numbers reared using natural parents and using Bengalese Finch foster-parents.

Total number of breeding pairs	119	
Mean numbers of pairs per breeder	6.0	
Total number of young reared to independence	1063	
Mean number of young per breeder	53.2	
Mean number of young per pair of Gouldian Finches	8.9	
Total number of young reared by natural parents	341	(32%)
Total number of young reared by Bengalese Finch foster-parents	732	(68%)

TABLE 6

The weights of Gouldian Finches reared by Bengalese Finch foster-parents and by their natural parents. Data from an article by F. Pickering (*The Grassfinch*, 1983, Vol. 7, No. 1, pp. 15–18).

		1980	
Birds	Rearing method	Number weighed	Mean weight
Immature birds	Bengalese Finch-reared	–	–
	Parent-reared	5	17.3g
Adult males	Bengalese Finch-reared	3	17.7g
	Parent-reared	7	18.9g
Adult females	Bengalese Finch-reared	3	15.0g
	Parent-reared	4	19.0g

but many small-scale breeders do nevertheless employ the foster-rearing method. Some rear all of their young under Bengalese Finches; others keep small numbers of them as 'insurance policies' in case their Gouldian Finches fail to rear young successfully. All but one out of 21 breeders who were questioned in a survey in 1983 foster-reared at least some young (Table 5) and, overall, about 70 per cent of their Gouldian Finches were reared under Bengalese Finches.

There is surprisingly little information on the quality of young produced by the foster-rearing and parent-rearing methods. Detailed comparisons are lacking but Mr F. Pickering presented some interesting information on the weights of individuals reared in these two ways (*The Grassfinch*, 1983, Vol. 7, No. 1, pp. 15–18). It can be seen from his data, which are summarised in Table 6, that differences in weights between the different categories are small. Nevertheless, they do exist, and there is some indication that parent-reared birds are heavier than foster-reared ones. The mean weight of all of the 62 parent-reared birds was 18.9g; that of the 29 foster-reared young was 17.8g. Further studies would be of great interest.

SOME DANGERS OF FOSTER-REARING

The most obvious danger in foster-rearing is in succumbing to the temptation

1981		1982	
Number weighed	*Mean weight*	*Number weighed*	*Mean weight*
5	19.5g	4	18.5g
6	19.5g	11	19.5g
6	17.0g	1	18.5g
4	18.5g	13	19.3g
6	18.0g	1	19.5g
3	17.2g	9	18.9g

to over-produce young in an effort to achieve quantity rather than quality. As the 'Japanese experience' has shown, this practice may result in short-term benefits for the breeders concerned but the production of birds of inferior quality is neither to their long-term advantage nor to that of aviculture as a whole.

An often-expressed fear concerns the problem of 'imprinting'. This process is one which is discussed in more detail in Chapter 10, but the basic worry is that foster-reared young will imprint on their Bengalese Finch foster-parents, and will subsequently refuse to pair and mate with members of their own species. Avicultural experience suggests, however, that, with current breeding practices, this is not a serious problem. Gouldian Finches reared by

TABLE 7

A survey of 21 Gouldian Finch breeders in the United Kingdom on procedures followed when natural Gouldian Finch parents fail to rear their young successfully. Responses were given to four questions.

Question	Number of answers		Percentage answering 'yes'
	Yes	No	
1) Do any of your pairs of Gouldian Finches fail to self-rear because they throw the young out of the nest?	12	9	57
2) Do any of your pairs of Gouldian Finches fail to self-rear because they desert clutches of eggs before they hatch?	12	9	57
3) Do you breed further from parents which fail for the reasons given in questions 1 and 2?	14	3	82
4) If the answer to question 3 is 'yes':			
Do you allow the natural (Gouldian Finch) parents to rear subsequent broods?	3	11	21
Do you foster-rear subsequent broods under Bengalese Finches?	11	3	79

foster-parents do pair successfully with their own kind, certainly as long as breeding pairs are caged separately from Bengalese Finches.

A problem which may be potentially more serious but which has been given less publicity, arises out of the habit of using Bengalese Finches to raise the young of Gouldian Finches which are themselves incapable of carrying out parental duties. More than half of the breeders questioned in the United Kingdom survey (see above) admitted to doing this when the natural parents failed to incubate their eggs or threw young out of the nest as soon as they hatched (Table 7). The danger is that these 'bad habits' are the result of genetic deficiencies and will therefore be transferred to the foster-reared young. They would be selected against and lost under natural conditions because birds with them would simply not breed successfully. Foster-rearing will, however, retain them in the population and even cause them to spread, increasing the fear of creating strains of Gouldian Finches which are incapable of rearing their own young. It would only be possible to propagate them by the use of Bengalese Finch foster-parents.

It is difficult, in any case, to justify the widespread use of foster-rearing on avicultural grounds. As Mr Derek Goodwin points out in his book *(Estrildid Finches of the World,* 1982, British Museum [Natural History] and Oxford University Press), aviculturists should aim to produce Gouldian Finches which will rear their own young in captivity as freely and successfully as Bengalese Finches.

The size and structure of a birdroom is obviously dependent on the number of birds which will be housed in it and, by no means less important, the aviculturist's personal circumstances. Various quarters have been adapted to this purpose, however, and birdrooms vary from converted sheds, workshops and garages, to spare attic rooms, cellars and purpose-built rooms (Fig. 15). Many different rooms will, in fact, satisfy the requirements as long as certain basic considerations are taken into account and sufficient thought is given to providing environmental conditions within which the birds will thrive.

WASHING AND STORAGE FACILITIES

It is wise to devote a special part of the room to storage. Shelves can be erected to accommodate spare feeding utensils, bird rings, bird nets, medicines and

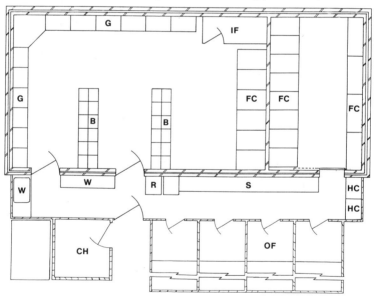

Fig. 15 *A plan of the birdroom belonging to M. E. Fidler. The room itself (excluding outdoor flights) measures 11 × 5.8m (36 × 19ft). It shows Gouldian Finch cages (G), Bengalese Finch cages (B), indoor flight (IF), flight cages (FC), storage area (S), washing and food preparation areas (W), outdoor flights (OF), central heating (CH), refrigerator (R) and hospital cages (HC).*

the innumerable other items which accumulate in the birdroom. Seed is bulkier and can be kept in plastic containers on the floor. Hot and cold running water, with a large sink (the larger the better) is highly desirable for washing and soaking soiled utensils and the trays of cages. Jobs, such as mixing soft food, require an easily-cleaned, hygienic working surface.

Where space is limited, these facilities can be provided outside the birdroom. They should not be given priority over one of the most important requirements of all: a chair or wooden bench at a central observation point from which the owner can watch his birds in comfort. Regular observations of the birds should be part of the daily maintenance schedule in order to check on the general health and condition of the stock. This is in any case the most enjoyable and instructive part of the hobby, and one which must not be ignored.

LIGHT

Ideally the birdroom should have a southerly or south-westerly aspect, with good window space so that the birds receive maximum benefit from natural daylight. It is important, nevertheless, not to devote too large an area to windows because the room will then be in danger of suffering from extremes in temperature, overheating in summer but cooling too rapidly in winter. Buildings such as greenhouses and glazed conservatories are generally unsuitable as birdrooms for these reasons. The provision of artificial light is essential in temperate parts of the world. It should be controlled by an automatic time switch so that 'daylength' can be increased during the short, dark days of winter. Thought must be given to the positions of lights so that the interiors of cages are well-illuminated. A central light tends to cast strong, deep shadows in them; side lights or batteries of roof lights which are positioned off-centre are generally more effective. It is advisable to provide a second source of lighting, a low-intensity night light. It prevents the birds from being plunged suddenly into darkness when the main lighting is switched off. Furthermore, the dim light reduces the chance of birds injuring themselves as a result of night frights. In total darkness, they react to sudden disturbances by flying about their cages in panic, crashing into the walls as they do so.

HEAT

Domestic, thermostatically-controlled fan-heaters are probably the easiest means of heating the birdroom. The correct temperature at which Gouldian Finches should be kept is a matter of considerable debate but, although acclimatised birds will tolerate lower temperatures, we recommend that the optimum temperature is between about 17 and 21°C (63–70°F). Below this, the birds utilise a considerable amount of energy simply in keeping the body warm, and we believe that their general condition and breeding performance suffer as a result. Since heating costs can be prohibitive, however, it is worth considering a plea from Mr G. Bailey *(The Grassfinch,* 1984, Vol. 8, pp. 37–39). He argues that one of the objectives of aviculturists should be to develop hardy strains of Gouldian Finches which can live and breed well in much lower temperatures than those provided for them in many birdrooms (see Chapter 9).

Birds lose heat much more rapidly in damp and draughty conditions than in dry, still air. It is important therefore to ensure that the room is draught-proof and dry. A maximum and minimum thermometer should be hung in the birdroom as a standard piece of equipment so that extremes in temperature can be monitored.

HUMIDITY

High relative humidities are needed during the breeding season because eggs lose water by evaporation and, in excessively dry air, this can cause the embryo to die before hatching (so-called 'dead in shell'). One advantage of gas heaters over electric ones is, in fact, that the former tend to keep the air moist (water vapour is released as the gas burns) whereas the latter dry it. Precise information is lacking but hatchability of eggs does not seem to suffer as long as humidity values are above about 50 per cent (some authors quote higher figures than this). The remedy, should there be a problem, depends on its severity and, again, the means of the aviculturist. The installation of a humidifier is an expensive answer but may be necessary to rectify extremely dry air. For less serious cases, moisture released by large potted plants kept in the birdroom or that evaporated from trays filled with gravel and water may be sufficient. (Open vessels containing water should be avoided, as escaped birds will attempt to drink from them and may drown.)

STRESS

Birds are unlikely to breed successfully unless they 'feel secure' in their flights or cages. Stress can result from a variety of different causes, such as overcrowding of birds, and infestations of vermin (see Chapter 8) and it is important to eliminate either possibility. Poor siting of cages also creates stress. The sudden appearance of the owner close to the front of the cage is frightening to the inhabitants so that cramped conditions, in which it is necessary to 'squeeze' past cages in order to service them, should be avoided. The birds benefit from having a good view of the birdroom from their cages. They then become accustomed to the owner's movements in the room, particularly if visits are made at the same times of day (e.g. in the early mornings and evenings) and largely ignore his or her presence. Some aviculturists make deliberate noises, such as knocking on the birdroom door or whistling, whenever they visit their birds, thereby warning them of their approach.

CAGES AND FLIGHTS

The numbers and sizes of cages and flights will be limited by the size of the birdroom. There are five possible types.

1) Breeding cages for pairs of Gouldian Finches (see Chapter 8).

2) Breeding cages for pairs of Bengalese Finches, should foster-rearing be contemplated (see Chapter 10).

3) Flight cages for housing either groups of Gouldian Finches which are coming into breeding condition or recently-weaned juveniles (see Chapter 8).

4) Outdoor flights, with access to the birdroom through closable bobholes. They can be used either for breeding Gouldian Finches out of doors (see Chapter 9) or allowing non-breeding birds to fly outside (see Chapter 8).

5) Indoor flights. These are an excellent general facility for colony breeding (see Chapter 9), keeping spare (non-breeding) stock during the winter, and for groups of juveniles.

CLEANLINESS AND HYGIENE

Too little attention is paid to hygiene by many aviculturists. The close, confined quarters of the birdroom present ideal conditions for the culture and growth of disease bacteria, and once they are established they can be difficult to eradicate. Chapter 14 is devoted to the treatment of illness, but prevention is always better than cure, and the observance of a few basic rules greatly reduces the chances of serious losses from disease.

The owner may be an agent for transmitting bacteria, and personal cleanliness is therefore important. The hands should be washed before cages are serviced and, if serious outbreaks of disease occur or are suspected, it may be advisable to wear rubber gloves. The main cause of illness in the birdroom is, however, the result of birds drinking water which has been fouled by their droppings or by picking up soiled, stale soft food from the floor of the cage. Regular changes of drinking water are essential, and soft food containers, drinking utensils and baths should be washed in diluted disinfectant every time they are used. They should also be positioned in cages so that they are not easily fouled (i.e. not directly beneath perches).

Cages should be washed and disinfected periodically and perches given an occasional wipe with a cloth soaked in disinfectant. The materials which are used to construct cages are important. Plastic-covered chipboard is excellent because it is so easily cleaned; plywood is cheaper but must be painted. All cages should be fitted with removable trays which are preferably made of galvanised sheet metal or aluminium. Both of these materials are more suitable than plywood, since they can be soaked in disinfectant and detergent. Sheets of newsprint paper, cut to appropriate sizes, make an excellent floor covering. A favoured and fast method of using them is to place a wadge of sheets, about 5mm ($\frac{1}{4}$in) thick, inside the tray and remove the top ones successively as they become soiled. Weekly cleaning is necessary if the more usual method of covering the tray with sand is employed.

The birdroom floor should be washed at weekly intervals. Solid, concrete floors are easily treated, and linoleum makes a good covering for a wooden floor. A concrete floor has the added advantage that it is vermin-proof. Unfortunately, the same cannot be said for wooden floors and measures should be taken to ensure that mice and rats are excluded from buildings which have them. One useful precaution is to sink an L-shaped piece of wire netting into the soil all round the birdroom and outside flights to a depth of about 30–45cm (12–18in). The L-shape increases its effectiveness by forming a horizontal ledge, at the maximum depth.

UTENSILS

Water fonts

The paramount need is to prevent the water from becoming fouled by droppings. Standard water fountains, which clip onto cage fronts, are good, but the water in them must be changed every one or two days. The drinkers which are supplied for rabbits and other rodents are used successfully by some breeders; each has a drinking nozzle which is closed by a moveable ball bearing. Automatic watering systems are potentially ideal but are not practical for the small-scale breeder, and some of those marketed are difficult to clean.

Seed hoppers

Open dishes are not recommended because the seed becomes contaminated with droppings. They are also labour-intensive since the seed husks must regularly be blown off them. Hoppers are preferred since they need to be filled infrequently, and there are designs available which fix on to cage fronts without special fitments. They are comparatively cheap, durable and easy to maintain.

Soft food feeders

Finger drawers used by canary breeders are often used and have the advantage that they hold about the right amount of soft food for one pair of Gouldian Finches for one day. The showcage drinkers which are supplied for budgerigars are also excellent containers.

Cuttlefish bone clips

These hold a piece of cuttlefish bone on to the inside of the cage front. Flaked cuttlefish bone is also supplied during the breeding season (see Chapter 8).

Seed cleaners and winnowers

A seed cleaner which operates from a vacuum cleaner can be effective and remove a considerable amount of dust from supposedly 'clean' seed. Commercial winnowers (i.e. machines which separate husks from uneaten seed) are available, but there is an added health risk in feeding 'recycled' seed to Gouldian Finches. An alternative solution is to feed the mix of husks and seed to other species, such as quail, which are efficient at picking out the edible remains.

6 PURCHASING, TRANSPORTING AND ACCLIMATISING BIRDS

Probably the most important advice that can be given to the beginner is not to be tempted to buy birds before everything is ready for them. It is imperative that suitable accommodation is available, for although Gouldian Finches are not difficult to keep in the right conditions they quickly succumb to inferior husbandry. It is advisable to make contact with experienced breeders and to join avicultural and bird societies, whose members are invariably keen to help newcomers. They are not only ideal people from whom to buy stock (see below) but are also well-qualified to give advice and help. If possible, visit their establishments and quiz them about their breeding methods.

PURCHASING

Consider what is regarded as a 'good bird' before buying and keep this in mind when going shopping. It should be possible to purchase stock from an established breeder, although it may be necessary to be patient; good birds are always in demand and there is often a waiting list. Remember that good birds will probably cost no more to buy than poor ones and will be no more expensive to feed and keep. They will, on the other hand, be far more likely to breed and remain in good condition. The best birds with which to start are freshly moulted juveniles which have yet to breed. By purchasing older ones you could be taking over someone else's problems. Stand and watch the birds you intend to buy. If they are listless and perch in a hunched posture with their feathers fluffed, reject them at any cost. The additional stress of moving birds which are in poor condition will probably kill them. Catch the birds under consideration and, when they are in the hand, check that their vents are clean and that they are plump around the breast. If the breastbone is prominent and sharp, return the bird to its cage, as it may be 'going light' (see Chapter 14). Check that the claws are not missing or malformed and that the beak is not overgrown. Do not buy a bird which is bald even if the vendor insists that this is due to plucking by its partner.

TRANSPORTING

Gouldian Finches are generally poor travellers. They are particularly prone to stress and this must be minimised. Providing the following rules are adhered to there should be few problems.

1) All carrying cases should be equipped with perches. Small cases are preferred to large ones because the birds may damage themselves when panicked if they are shipped in large cages. It is important, nevertheless, that they are not overcrowded.

2) It is necessary to ensure that the birds have adequate light, ventilation, food and water while travelling. Because of the Gouldian Finch's method of drinking, water can be provided by using a piece of soaked plastic sponge from which they will suck moisture.

3) The birds must be kept warm, free from draughts and away from car exhaust, and other fumes, during the journey.

4) Birds which are expected to travel long distances (over 24 hours) can be tranquillised in order to reduce the stress factor. One way of doing this is to dissolve two (2mg) tablets of a tranquilliser in a pint of warm water. This solution is given to the birds in place of normal drinking water the day before shipment.

ACCLIMATISING NEW ARRIVALS

The first few days when the birds are housed in strange surroundings are also stressful ones for them. The following rules will help to avoid losses.

1) Stressed birds are susceptible to bacterial infection so that their drinking water should be boiled for the first three days. Phase in unboiled, local tap water over the next five days.

2) Keep birds which have travelled long distances on the tranquilliser for about two days, until the effects of stress have worn off.

3) Do not subject the new arrivals to unnecessary noise or disturbance.

4) Keep the birdroom warm, at about 30°C (85°F) for the first few days, gradually reducing it to the temperature at which it is normally kept.

5) Scatter seed on the floor and put a dish of water in the middle of the cage until there is no doubt that the birds have found the correct feeding and watering points.

6) If possible, quarantine the new birds away from other stock, until it is clear that they are not suffering from any diseases.

7 NUTRITION

Nutrition is one aspect of bird keeping which cannot be ignored at any cost. The primary task of aviculturists must be to provide their birds with the full range of foods needed to keep them healthy and permit them to breed. Examples of the consequences of deficient diets on mortalities of juvenile Gouldian Finches during the first moult have already been given in Chapter 4. Another particularly striking example of the importance of diet is described in an article by Mr E. Baxter *(Australian Aviculture,* October 1951, pp. 122–123). Like many Australian breeders, Mr Baxter normally paired his birds in December. He relates how they started to breed well in the 1950/51 season and that, by late January, at least 15 of his pairs had young in the nest. Greenfood and seeding grasses were in extremely short supply in the early spring of that year, however, and the breeding birds were receiving relatively little of them in their diet. Evidently, as a result of this, most of the nests failed before the young fledged from them; some of them were deserted and the young from others were 'thrown out' by their parents. In the end, only two young from the whole of the first round reached maturity. A complete turn round of events for the second brood leaves little doubt that an inadequate diet was the problem. Greenfood and seeding grasses were abundant by this time, and the birds were then given them daily. Nest after nest was reared successfully, and 62 youngsters were reared overall. The supply of natural 'greens' ran out for the third round and this too was relatively unsuccessful; 17 young were reared from it.

Birds living under natural conditions select balanced diets from the variety of foods available to them. Unfortunately, it is not usually possible to supply captive birds with exactly the same foods as those that are taken in the wild, and the challenge to aviculture is to find suitable alternatives. These must not only be acceptable to the birds but must also provide them with the nutrients needed for their survival. This is a problem the solution to which requires an understanding of bird nutrition, together with a mixture of intelligent guesswork and good practical bird-keeping. The first part of this chapter is therefore devoted to the nutrient requirements of the balanced diet and the latter part to the ways in which these needs can be satisfied in captive Gouldian Finches.

THE BALANCED DIET

The bird's diet must include the following nutrients.

Carbohydrates

These substances include sugars and starch. They are the primary sources of energy which is needed to keep the body warm and fuel the muscular activity involved in flight and other movement. Grass seeds are particularly rich in them. Canary seed, for instance, contains about 67 per cent carbohydrates, 17 per cent proteins, 7 per cent fats and 9 per cent water. Millet contains 73 per cent carbohydrates, 14 per cent proteins, 5 per cent fats and 8 per cent water. As long as seeds of these kinds are always available for finches, they should never suffer from carbohydrate deficiency.

Fats

They are readily stored in the body and are also sources of energy. In fact, they yield more energy for the equivalent weight than carbohydrates. The metabolism of a gram of fat yields 9.4 Calories, whereas that of a gram of carbohydrate yields only 4.2 Calories. Fats are, however, less easily digested than carbohydrates and finches utilise them in relatively small quantities.

Proteins

These compounds are vital for growth because they are the major components of the body's organs, including the skin, feathers, muscles, eyes, nervous system etc. Their molecules are complex and each is made up of units called amino acids. Animals can synthesise their own proteins in the body but only if certain of these amino acids (so-called essential ones) are available in the diet. Many animal foods, such as live insects, milk and mashed boiled eggs, are excellent sources of amino acids. So too are germinating seeds, because the proteins stored in the dry seed are broken down into their constituent amino acids as a result of the chemical changes that accompany germination. Similarly, amino acids are involved in the growth and development of seeds, and seeding grasses are also rich in them. Wheatgerm extract makes an excellent substitute in the absence of seeding grasses.

Vitamins

They are required in only tiny amounts by the body. Their importance to it is nevertheless such that a diet which is complete in every respect except that it lacks one of them can result in unhealthy birds and, in extreme cases, their death. When vitamins were first discovered and isolated, they were known by the letters of the alphabet (Vitamin A, Vitamin B etc.) but, as more and more of them have been found, this convention has been partly dropped. Nowadays, their chemical names are often used instead. This applies in particular to some which are not single vitamins but whole complexes of them. The Vitamin B complex is a good example. Table 8 lists some of the

TABLE 8
Some of the important vitamins for birds, the foods in which they occur and the effects when the diet is deficient in them.

	Vitamin	*Rich food source*	*Effects of deficiency*
A	retinol	green food	low resistence to disease; skin and eyes become dry
B (complex)	biotin	yeast	dermatitis; poor hatchability of eggs
	cholin	milk	perosis
	folaccin	green food; milk	anaemia and poor growth
	niacin	green food; milk	poor feather production
	riboflavin	green food	poor hatchability of eggs; poor growth
	cobalamin	liver; animal foods	poor hatchability of eggs; poor growth
D_3	cholecalciferol	manufactured in sunlight	poor bone formation; thin shelled eggs (egg-binding)
E	toccopherol	grass seeds; green food	poor health; poor hatchability

more important ones and indicates the likely effects of deficiencies in them. This information is based primarily on research on the domestic fowl but, although caution should be exercised in generalising the findings from one species to others, it will almost certainly hold good for the Gouldian Finch as well. Vitamins occur in a variety of natural foods, such as greenfood, milk and yeast. They can also be provided from artificial sources such as supplements which can be added to drinking water and 'soft food mixes'. Table 9 shows the constituents of one widely used soft food.

Vitamin D_3, which is required for egg-shell production and bone formation, is exceptional in that it can be synthesised in the bird's skin. This only occurs, however, in the presence of the ultraviolet rays of natural sunlight. Artificial light from most sources contains little ultraviolet and birds which are kept indoors throughout the year have no chance of manufacturing it. It follows that, unless birds are allowed to fly in the outside flights for several months of the year, Vitamin D_3 must be provided in the diet. Females have a particularly high Vitamin D_3 requirement during egg-laying, and the first symptom of

TABLE 9
The mineral salt and vitamin content of one rearing food *Cédé-eivoer*, which is available in Europe. The content of two amino acids, methionine and lysine, is also shown. Similar rearing foods are available in other parts of the world.

Substance	Quantity	Substance		Quantity	
Manganese	80 mg	Vitamins	A	19500	I.U.
Iodine	1 mg		B_1	12	mg
Cobalt	18 mg		B_2	38	mg
Zinc	58 mg		B_6	2	mg
Copper	5 mg		B_{12}	0.01	mg
Magnesium	125 mg		C	4	mg
Iron	29 mg		D_3	2000	I.U.
			K_3	2	mg
		Pantothine		55	mg
		Niacin		100	mg
DL Methionine	500 mg	Cholin		475	mg
L Lysine	1150 mg	Biotin		0.4	mg

deficiency is likely to be soft-shelled eggs, and egg-binding as a result of their inability to lay them.

Mineral salts

These substances, like vitamins, are essential in the diet in very small amounts. They are present in many natural foods, such as greenfood (see e.g. Table 10), and unnatural sources, such as soft food (see Table 9) and mineralised grit. Mr B. Hislop *(The Grassfinch,* 1983, Vol. 7, pp. 41–43) lists the following in one proprietary brand of grit: potassium, calcium, phosphorus, sodium, magnesium, manganese and iron. The body needs them for various functions and some examples will illustrate their importance.

TABLE 10
The analysis of three greenfoods which are suitable for feeding to Gouldian Finches. The values are based on about 0.4kg by weight of the edible parts of each of the plants (information from T. Bucci, *AFA Watchbird Magazine*, December 1980/January 1981, pp. 4–8).

	Dandelion	*Chicory*	*Lettuce*
Protein	14 g	5 g	4 g
Fat	3 g	2 g	1 g
Carbohydrate	40 g	15 g	9 g
Calcium	842 mg	750 mg	158 mg
Phosphorus	315 mg	322 mg	118 mg
Iron	14 mg	70 mg	1 mg
Potassium	1900 mg	1906 mg	650 mg
Vitamin A	67970 I.U.	32160 I.U.	8060 I.U.
Niacin	3.3 mg	0.0 mg	1.3 mg
Riboflavin	0.7 mg	0.0 mg	0.3 mg
Thiamin	0.9 mg	0.8 mg	0.1 mg

Calcium is required in especially large quantities by the egg-laying female for egg-shell formation; cuttlefish bone and sometimes crushed egg shells are usually provided to satisfy this need in cage birds. Phosphorus is also needed for egg-shell formation and, together with calcium, is a vital constituent of the blood and is also needed for bone development; iodine and manganese are important for egg-production in females; sodium and chlorine are involved in growth and digestive processes and in the correct functioning of the blood; copper is required for the manufacture of the black pigment eumelanin; and cobalt is needed for the synthesis of Vitamin B_{12} (cobalamin).

Grit

This is not strictly a component of the diet because it is of no nutritive value (except for the added mineral salts; see above). Seed-eating birds need it, however, as an aid to digestion in the part of the stomach known as the gizzard. Here food is ground with particles of grit and broken into small pieces. This enables the digestive juices to act more effectively on it, and for the bird to derive greater benefit from its food.

Plate 1 *A male black-headed Gouldian Finch.*

Plate 2 *Juvenile Gouldian Finches.*

Plate 3 *Male red-headed (right) and yellow-headed (left) Gouldian Finches.*

Plate 4 *A dry river bed during the dry season in northern Australia. Water becomes restricted to a few pools and most of these eventually dry out.*

Plate 5 *Open woodland during the dry season in northern Australia. The* Eucalyptus *trees are well spaced out and have a dense ground cover of grasses between them.*

Plate 6 *A female red-headed Gouldian Finch whose belly feathers have been parted revealing the brood patch.*

Plate 7 (opposite) *A pair of white-breasted Gouldian Finches.*

Plate 8 *A male black-headed, dilute-backed Gouldian Finch. Since this variety does not manufacture the black pigment eumelanin in its feathers, the head is grey.*

Plate 9 *A blue-backed Gouldian Finch, a mutation which has appeared in Holland.*

Plate 10 *A male blue-breasted Gouldian Finch contrasted with a normal male.*

Plate 11 *A male yellow-headed, white-breasted, pastel Gouldian Finch.*

Plate 12 *Three nestlings about 12 days after hatching. One is a dilute-backed and, due to its lack of eumelanin, is quite different from its nest-mates, even at this age.*

NUTRIENT NEEDS AT DIFFERENT STAGES IN THE LIFE CYCLE

The food requirements of birds are not always the same. Adults which are neither breeding nor moulting need diets which are rich in carbohydrates because they spend most of their time engaged in energy-demanding activities such as flight. Since they are not growing, their protein, vitamin and mineral salt requirements are relatively small. These substances are, however, in great demand at three other stages in their lives.

First, the developing chick must be supplied with a diet which is rich in all nutrients, especially proteins, so that it can grow. Carbohydrates are relatively less important at this time because the chick expends little energy in movement.

Second, adult birds require a nutrient rich diet when they breed in order to manufacture their reproductive cells (eggs or sperms). This need is particularly important in the adult female since her eggs must contain all the

TABLE 11
The amounts of essential amino acids which are used by domestic fowl at three stages in the life cycle: the non-breeding adult, the young chick and the egg-laying hen. The figures are relative amounts using the quantity of threonine as unity (after Fischer, 1972).

Amino acids	Non-breeding adult	Young chick	Egg-laying hen
Arginine	1.6	1.5	1.8
Histidine	0.0	0.5	0.5
Lysine	0.4	1.4	1.4
Isoleucine	1.0	0.9	1.4
Leucine	1.7	1.8	1.9
Valine	0.8	1.3	1.5
Tryptophan	0.2	0.2	0.3
Methionine	1.0	0.5	0.7
Phenylalanine	0.4	0.8	1.2
Glycine	0.0	0.5	0.0
Threonine	1.0	1.0	1.0
Total	8.1	10.4	11.7

substances required for the healthy development of the embryo for its first two weeks of life (until it hatches and is fed by its parents).

Third, the moult also places heavy demands on the need for nutrients. The protein requirement is particularly great because feathers consist of about 90 per cent protein. There is, in addition, a 10 to 20 per cent increase in the metabolism of carbohydrates and fats during the moult. This is due, at least in part, to the need to keep the body warm when moulting temporarily reduces the insulating effectiveness of its covering of feathers.

The way in which the amino acid (protein) need of the domestic fowl changes at different stages in its life is illustrated by the information presented in Table 11. The young chick requires larger amounts of essential amino acids than the adult both overall and in the case of specific ones, such as histidine, lysine, valine, phenylalanine and glycine. The adult requirement is much greater during egg-production and, if anything, is larger even than that of the growing chick.

SATISFYING NUTRIENT NEEDS UNDER NATURAL CONDITIONS

Birds are adapted to select balanced diets in nature but food availability often changes in different seasons. It is not surprising to find, however, that they exploit these changes by performing particularly demanding activities such as breeding, at times when there are abundant supplies of nutrient-rich foods. Most species in temperate latitudes breed in spring and early summer when they can feed on the hordes of insects and other small animals and growing vegetation (e.g. seeding grasses). The Gouldian Finch, like most other inhabitants of tropical and sub-tropical climates, breeds in the wet season when there is a similar explosion of protein-rich foods (see Chapters 2 and 3). It is also important for birds to avoid the combined stresses of moulting and breeding at the same time. The Gouldian Finch, for instance, moults after the completion of breeding activities. Sometimes, first year juveniles are still in the moult at the start of the breeding season and, in such cases, moulting is interrupted and inhibited. These birds nest partly in juvenile and partly in adult plumage and then re-commence and complete the moult after they have finished breeding.

SATISFYING THE FEEDING REQUIREMENTS OF THE GOULDIAN FINCH IN CAPTIVITY

The usual practice in feeding Gouldian Finches, and that recommended here, is to simulate the pattern of feeding shown by this species in the wild. They are given an austere diet, which is based on dry seed, during the non-breeding season but an enriched one during the breeding season. The full year's schedule is shown in Table 12.

Curiously, the Gouldian Finch is often reluctant to take insects in captivity so that it is necessary to provide alternatives to the termites, on which they feed extensively under natural conditions, by some other means. The three most common alternatives are: germinating (soaked) seed, seeding grasses (as in Mr Baxter's case; see above) and a suitable soft food mix. Many breeders give their birds more than one of these foods during the breeding season but others achieve good success with only one of them. Our own recommendations are given in Chapter 8.

TABLE 12
The Gouldian Finch's feeding schedule for breeding and non-breeding seasons.

Non-breeding Season	
Always available:	Dry seed mix
	Mineralised grit
	Cuttlefish bone
Supplied regularly:	Vitamin supplement
	Green food
Breeding Season	
Always available:	Dry seed mix
	Mineralised grit
	Cuttlefish bone
Once or twice daily:	Soft food mix
	and/or
	Seeding grasses
	and/or
	Germinating (soaked) seed
Supplied regularly:	Vitamin supplement
	Green food

The remainder of this chapter gives further details of the foods which are included in the diet.

The Standard Seed Mix

This forms the staple diet throughout the year and is the main source of carbohydrates and fats. The recommended mix is as follows:

25 per cent canary seed

25 per cent white millet

25 per cent panicum millet

25 per cent plate millet

Millet spray, although not essential, is a welcome addition. The best method of feeding it is to fix the ends of 3 or 4 stalks together with masking or adhesive tape, and then to hang them over a perch or hook. The birds will spend hours climbing over it to feed, evidently giving themselves a great deal of pleasure in the process. Gouldian Finches will also accept Japanese millet and white millet. Incidentally, Teague believed that white millet poisoned his birds, a theory which has now been thoroughly disproved.

Germinating (Soaked) Seed

The germination process is initiated by soaking seeds in water. The important chemical changes, which enrich the seed as a food, occur within two to three days of the start of germination, and the seed should be fed to the birds at this stage. It is not necessary to wait for the seed to sprout. This takes much longer and, in any case, feeding sprouted seed is in effect an expensive way of providing greenfood. The following system of soaking seed is recommended.

1) Place the seed in a container and cover it with water. Fit the lid on to the container and leave it in a warm place, such as the top of a central heating boiler, for 12 hours. Seeds germinate more rapidly between about 25 and 30°C (77 and 85°F).

2) At the end of this period, empty the seed into a sieve, and rinse it thoroughly with cold water. Replace the damp seed in the container. Fit the lid into position and put the container back into the warm place for another 12 hours.

3) Now remove the lid, allowing surplus water to evaporate, while

germination continues. Leave the seed like this for a day, checking that it does not dry out completely. It is now ready to be fed to the birds.

The favoured seeds to soak are millets, including spray millet, although the standard seed mix can also be used. A word of warning is necessary, however. Soaked seed can become foul. Healthy soaked seed has a characteristic smell of fermentation. A decidedly unpleasant smell indicates that it has 'gone off'. It should then be thrown away. If you have soaked too much seed, the surplus can be kept in the refrigerator. The cooling effect arrests germination, without killing the seed.

Greenfood

There are several excellent wild plants, although care must be taken to collect them from unpolluted sources. Choose places which have not been contaminated by dogs, insecticides, fertilisers or motor traffic. As an extra precaution, rinse collected plants under the cold tap before offering them to your birds.

Chickweed *(Stellaria media)* is highly nutritious and probably the most popular greenfood. Gouldian Finches enjoy the seeding heads, and avidly eat the flowers and the leaves. Dandelion *(Taraxacum officinale)* will be eaten, although in smaller quantities. It is fed complete with root and leaf, and the birds will spend hours pecking over it. They appear to enjoy it when it is hung in the cage and this also prevents it from becoming soiled too rapidly. The leaves and flowers of both red and white clover *(Trifolium repens)* are readily accepted.

One way of eliminating the risk of contaminated greenfood is to grow it in the garden. Lettuce is the obvious vegetable to offer, and chicory is also highly beneficial.

Seeding grasses can be collected and fed to the birds in abundance. Unfortunately, they are not available to those European breeders, and others living in temperate climates, who breed their birds indoors during the winter.

Soft Food Mix

A formula developed by one of the authors (Mike Fidler), which is rich in proteins, mineral salts and vitamins, is as follows:

4 tablespoons of canary rearing food (see e.g. Table 9)
1 tablespoon of wheatgerm extract

1 teaspoon of brewer's yeast

1 teaspoon of multi-mineral powder.

The mineral powder is one used by farmers to supplement cattle feed. The mixture should be moistened lightly with milk or water until a fluffy mash is obtained, and this should be crumbly, but not sticky to touch. Milk has the advantage as an additive that it is highly nutritious itself but it has the disadvantage that it goes sour within a relatively short period of time.

Vitamin Supplements

There are many vitamin preparations on the market which can be added to the birds' drinking water. Some breeders use cod liver oil to satisfy the Vitamin D_3 need. Dry seed mix is mixed with oil and then given to the birds in place of their normal seed mix. Cod liver oil is extremely rich in this vitamin but it must not be allowed to go rancid. This not only destroys its Vitamin D_3 content, but, worse still, inactivates Vitamin E if it is absorbed into the bird's body. Overall, the use of cod liver oil should perhaps be avoided, except in cases in which severe deficiency symptoms have already appeared. The provision of a vitamin supplement, which is rich in D_3, at regular intervals throughout the year should prevent this situation from arising, even in birds which never fly in outside aviaries.

PERSUADING BIRDS TO TAKE UNFAMILIAR FOODS

Birds are sometimes reluctant to sample a new food when it is provided for them. It is wise to persevere and to supply it regularly, however. Once one member of a group takes a liking to it, others copy it and the habit soon spreads. Some breeders report that Gouldian Finches are quick to explore foods which are presented to them at perch height rather than on the floor of the cage. They argue that this is the 'preferred feeding height' for a species which feeds from grass pannicles in the wild and does not normally take food from the ground. Mr Robert G. Black *(Nutrition of Finches and Other Cage Birds,* 1981, printed by Copple House Printing & Binding, Lakemont, Georgia) recommends the practice of temporarily removing all foods, apart from the unfamiliar one, from the cage. In this way, the inhabitants are more-or-less forced into sampling it. Obviously care is needed to ensure that the birds are not left without their normal foods for unnecessarily long periods.

8 CAGE BREEDING

Gouldian Finches come into breeding condition during the wet season in the wild (see Chapter 3) and this is the only time of year at which they attempt to breed. Breeding condition, however, implies much more than being in good health. It involves a series of changes within the body which prepare the animal for nesting. The process starts in the male with the enlargement and development of the testes, which until now have been small and inactive. They produce sperms and, at the same time, release male hormones into the blood. These stimulate reproductive behaviour: singing and courtship are two expressions of it in the male Gouldian Finch. The ovaries of the female also develop as she comes into breeding condition. They too secrete hormones and eggs mature in them.

These internal changes within the bird's body occur in response to changes in the environment which signal the approach of suitable conditions for breeding. The trigger in many birds which nest during the spring and early summer in temperate parts of the world is the gradual increase in daylength (i.e. daylight) as the short days of winter give way to the longer ones of spring. There is much less seasonal change in daylength near the equator, however, and the development of breeding condition in most tropical species is triggered by different cues. The sudden flush of vegetation and super-abundance of food that occurs in the rainy season stimulates it in many of them but some species, which live in areas of unpredictable rainfall, respond to the rain itself. Zebra Finches and parrots, which live in the arid, desert regions of central Australia, for instance, are always in a state of readiness to breed. They may wait for months or years without doing so but go to nest immediately it rains.

The Gouldian Finch lives in areas of predictable climate and, although the trigger which brings them into breeding condition is unknown, experience with captive birds suggest that it may occur in response to the change to the protein-rich diet of seeding grasses and termites in the wet season. It can be bred at any time of year in captivity by bringing it into the right condition with the provision of protein-rich soft food.

There are basically two ways in which Gouldian Finches are bred in captivity: either they are isolated in pairs in separate cages (or flights); or they are bred on a colony system in which several pairs are housed together in the same flight. This chapter is concerned with the first of these methods: cage breeding. Colony breeding is the subject of Chapter 9. Cage breeding has the advantages that it is economical on space, enables matings between birds to be controlled and, with some notable exceptions, is more successful in terms of numbers of young produced than colony breeding. It is widely practised by aviculturists in Europe and the United States, particularly by those who breed their birds in indoor birdrooms during the winter. There are, nevertheless, many differences (albeit often small ones) in the ways in which individual breeders rear their birds, each tending to swear by the particular idiosyncracies of his or her own methods. Our objective here is to present the details of one well-proven method which has been developed by one of the authors (Mike Fidler) over a period of more than twenty years and is known to be successful. The technique described is one in which the parents are allowed to rear their own young. The breeding potential of stock can be increased by fostering clutches of Gouldian Finch eggs under Bengalese Finches, and the ways of doing this are described later in Chapter 10. The potential dangers of foster-rearing have, however, been expounded in Chapter 4, and we recommend that it is only used after careful consideration.

BRINGING BIRDS INTO BREEDING CONDITION

Most breeders allow their birds to fly in large flights during the period when they are not breeding from them. The diet at this time is the relatively austere one described in Chapter 7. This treatment is important because it gives the birds a chance to mature or to recover fully from any previous breeding activities, and to moult. Ideally, they fly in outside aviaries through the warm summer months so that they are in excellent general condition, ready to be brought back into the birdroom in the autumn. Once this has been done, the first priority is to bring the birds into breeding condition. It is customary to cage the males and females separately while doing so, thereby breaking, or weakening, any pair-bonds which may have formed while they have been flying communally, and accelerating the development of breeding condition. The birds are now provided with daily rations of the nutrient-rich soft food mix described in Chapter 7, and ample supplies of cuttlefish bone. The soft food may be taken in only small quantities but it is nevertheless a most important addition to the diet. 'Climatic' conditions in the birdroom are also adjusted in preparation for breeding, by using artificial light to supplement the ever-shortening natural daylight hours of winter, giving and maintaining a regime of 15 hours of light and 9 hours of darkness, and maintaining the temperature at a minimum of about 21°C (70°F).

CAGES

The sizes of breeding cages are unimportant, as long as they are not less than 60×45×45cm (24×18×18in). Each starts the season with a thorough clean, receiving treatment with a strong non-residual disinfectant and, where necessary, an insecticide. The floor of each cage is covered either with absorbent paper or washed sand, together with a handful of oystershell grit and one of grated cuttlefish bone. This method of providing grit and cuttlefish is preferred to that of supplying it in pots, since the birds appear to enjoy it more as they pick over it, and it helps to keep them occupied and active. Perches are between 6 and 10mm ($\frac{1}{4}$ and $\frac{3}{8}$in) in thickness, and are roughened by dragging a fine-toothed tenon saw along their lengths. They are fixed firmly from the front to the back of the cage. It is important that the birds can secure a good grip on their perches because, contrary to popular belief, matings between captive birds often take place on the perches or on the floor of the cage. (Copulation is said to occur in the nest in the wild; see Chapter 3.) Smooth or unsteady perches may lead to unsuccessful attempts to mate, and therefore to the production of infertile eggs. A common mistake is to fit too many perches in the cage, but there is a need for only two. One should be positioned at one end of the cage, close to the ceiling but leaving adequate head and tail space, and the other at the other end of the cage, near the floor. Such positioning ensures that the birds will use the full space available to them in the cage and that they will have to 'fly hard' from the bottom to the top perch, getting plenty of exercise in the process.

There has been considerable controversy in the past over the type of nest box most preferred by the Gouldian Finch. In reality, they will use almost any kind of semi-enclosed nesting receptacle, including the nest boxes normally supplied to budgerigars. The most convenient ones are square (11cm or $4\frac{1}{2}$in) with a half-open front (Fig. 16). If these are fixed externally on to the wire fronts of each cage, they can be inspected easily with minimal disturbance to breeding pairs.

A handful of soft dried grass and a small bundle of coconut fibre (about 18–23cm; 7–9in) is placed on the floor of the cage, away from the perches

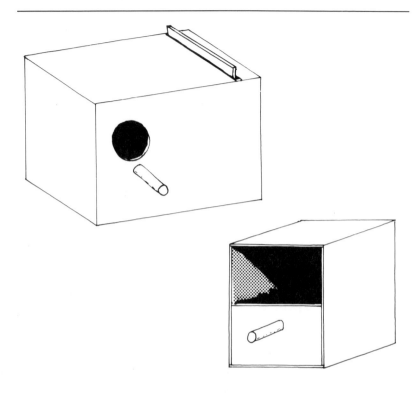

Fig. 16 *Two types of nest boxes which will be used by Gouldian Finches. The half-open box-type is recommended for use in cages.*

where it could be soiled by droppings. Some nesting material is pushed into the nest box itself, and is formed into a nest with the fist. The male adds further material and improves on the layout of the nest later, but the extra help seems to act as a stimulus for him to start nest-building.

RECOGNISING BREEDING CONDITION

The best time to set up pairs is when they are in peak breeding condition. They probably reach this about two to six weeks after being brought back into the birdroom. General indicators of condition are that the birds are bright and active; they look as if they are raring to go! More specific signs are as follows.

Females

They 'bounce' from perch to perch, and often alight on the cage front. Repeated contact calls are given, evidently to the males. A characteristic posture is often adopted in which the female crouches on the floor of the cage or on a perch, raises the wings slightly away from the body and performs rapid shimmering movements with them. The tail may, at the same time, be twisted sideways. The female's beak tends to blacken, particularly in black-headed individuals, as she comes into breeding condition, although blackening is not achieved fully in some birds until as late as the second round of eggs.

Males

Like females, they become hyperactive and go through the wing-shimmering routine. Some of them also perform the act of twirling, in which the head is

Fig. 17 *A male Gouldian Finch in the act of twirling.*

jerked backwards towards the tail (Fig. 17), an act which was once regarded as a symptom of vitamin deficiency. Males in breeding condition spend a lot of their time singing, and the beak becomes pearly white.

INTRODUCING PARTNERS: COMPATIBLE AND INCOMPATIBLE PAIRS

It is usual to introduce the male into the breeding cage first, and the female follows a matter of hours or days later. Many breeders watch the reactions of the male and female towards one another closely on introduction for signs that they are compatible. It is common experience that birds which perform their courtship displays to one another turn out to be good breeding pairs.

The male often shows his willingness to pair by displaying within the first few minutes of introduction. Frequently he beak-wipes before going into his head-shaking routine and then the bobbing display (see Chapter 3). The female indicates acceptance by twisting her tail towards the male (Fig. 10) by beak-wiping and, sometimes, by performing the bobbing display herself. Pairs may repeat the display several times. They also perch close together when inactive and the female tends to follow the male about the cage whenever he moves his perching place.

Incompatibility is signalled by aggression, such as beak-fencing between birds, perching well apart and general disinterest in one another. Birds which behave in these ways are usually separated and tried with other mates.

The male is the first to inspect the nest box, after the initial courtship routine. He usually peers into it from the top of the box without entering it. The female perches nearby, and may make her own inspection soon afterwards. Commonly, the male picks up nesting materials and, after carrying them round the cage, drops them. He then enters the nest for the first time.

The male builds the nest and, although the female watches his activities, she is not permitted to enter the box in the early stages. Once the nest is complete, however, she enters and the pair spends some time together inside it.

EGG-LAYING, HATCHING AND REARING

Eggs are usually produced within 15 to 21 days of the introduction of a compatible pair, although some pairs (probably those which are not in full breeding condition) may take longer than this. Incubation may start after the third egg, well before the full clutch has been laid. Fertile eggs become pinkish due to the formation of the embryo's blood vessels after five days, and then opaque, with a characteristically solid appearance, as the embryo develops. Hatching usually takes place on the 15th to 16th day.

Soft food is now supplied twice a day and the amount is gradually increased as the chick grows, ensuring that there is always as much as the parents are prepared to take. The second feeding should be in the early evening so that the chicks are fed and their crops filled with it before nightfall. Soaked seed should also be given from the 12th day until weaning.

Most domestic strains of Gouldian Finches will normally tolerate daily nest box inspections, even in the period immediately after hatching, and, if the boxes are slotted into the fronts of cages as recommended here, such interference causes little harm. Parents are otherwise disturbed as little as possible for the first few days after hatching, since this is the most vulnerable time for the chicks. Most of the problems are over if they can survive it without mishap. There is a school of thought which advocates no inspections at all and it is perhaps as well to heed this advice if members of a pair are nervous or flighty, or if the nest box is in an awkward position in the cage. The purpose of the inspection is not, in any case, to satisfy idle curiosity. It is done primarily to check the condition of the chicks. Their crops should be full, and their skins smooth and shiny with a blackish sheen; their droppings should be reasonably firm and part should be black, contrasting with the other part which should be white. Obviously any dead chicks should be removed from the nest.

The chicks fledge at approximately 21 days of age and, having done so, they do not normally return to the nest, even to roost (there are exceptions). Any chicks which are more than a day later than their nest mates in fledging should be placed on the floor of the cage. Failure to do so may result in the parents neglecting either the chicks in the nest box or those which have already fledged. Late youngsters are often poor fliers and may spend their first day or so on the floor of the cage. In this situation, the top perch in the cage is lowered to within a few inches of the floor. This keeps the parents within close proximity of all of their chicks and the begging calls from those on the floor are more likely to stimulate them to feed their offspring. The nest box is removed, thereby discouraging the parents from starting the next brood too early, and diverting their attention from feeding the first round of chicks.

Chicks will start feeding themselves when they are about 32 days old, at which stage they readily take soaked millet spray placed on the floor of the cage. They are usually removed from their parents at, or soon after, the 35th day, when they are self-sufficient. They are placed in cages, taking care to avoid over-crowding. Six can be housed in a cage measuring 75×45×45cm (30×18×18in). It is valuable if one of these is an older bird since the younger ones follow it to the food and water. Soaked seed and soft food are still included in the diet.

GETTING THROUGH THE MOULT

Chicks which are about two and a half months old are transferred to flights. If the breeding season has been a successful one, it may be difficult to avoid over-crowding the birds, simply because there are insufficient flights for all of them. It is nevertheless possible to house as many as 50 juveniles together in flights measuring 3×1.5×2m (10×5×7ft) as long as precautions are taken to reduce stress and harassment. One way of doing this is to divide the perches into a series of sections about 25cm (10in) long with cardboard or plastic dividers. Each section provides sufficient room for two birds to perch without interference from others.

Hygiene is vitally important for juvenile survival, particularly if large numbers of birds are housed together; the floors of the flights and the perches must be cleaned regularly. Soft food is provided until the moult is complete but only once per day, together with soaked seed and greenfood.

KEEPING RECORDS AND RINGING BIRDS

It is essential to keep good records, and an ideal way of doing this is to use cards which are prepared by some bird societies for this purpose (Fig. 18). These can be fixed to the cages and information added to them as it becomes available. The records may not be immediately useful but become invaluable if, for example, breeding performance is one of the criteria which is used to select the following year's breeding stock. Individuals are identified by means of closed aluminium rings. Coloured plastic rings, which are available in an assortment of colours and combinations of colours, are also used and have the advantage that they permit identification without having to catch the birds.

Gouldian Finch nestlings should be 'close-ringed' when they are between 7

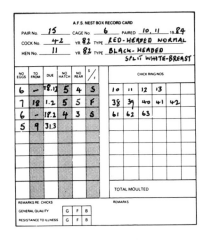
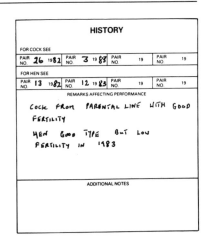

Fig. 18 *The two sides of one of the record cards produced by the Australian Finch Society (UK).*

and 9 days old. At this stage the foot is large enough to keep the ring on to the leg but small enough to allow ringing to occur. The nestling is placed in the palm of the left hand and the index finger and thumb hold the knee joint of the leg which is to be ringed. A firm grip above and below the joint causes the limb to straighten and the bird reacts by straightening out its toes. The ring is now threaded carefully over the front three toes (which can be moistened with saliva or water) and pushed and twisted gently on to the ball of the foot. The hand grip is now changed. The tips of the toes are held with the free hand, while the index finger and thumb manipulate the ring over the ball of the foot and on up the leg. The one remaining toe is forced backwards as the ring passes over it. It must be freed from the ring, either with a matchstick or by teasing it out with finger and thumb nails.

PROBLEMS

No eggs

If there are no eggs about 3 to 4 weeks after the introduction of a pair into the breeding cage, introduce another male (spare males should be kept for this purpose). The female will not normally pair with him but his presence usually spurs the residents into nesting activity. This is probably because the first male now has to compete with a rival, and the female is stimulated by the attention of two males. It is usual that, within a few days, both members of the pair reject the intruder and react aggressively towards him. He should then be removed. Eggs can be expected 8 to 14 days after his rejection.

Failure to nest after this treatment may indicate that the pair is under stress. This could be caused by too many nest box inspections, too much general disturbance in the birdroom, strangers coming into it, or bad siting or insecure fixing of the nest box. Separate and isolate members of the pair, if all else fails, and re-pair them two or three weeks later. If there is still no success, try them with new partners.

Nestlings thrown out of the nest

The culprit is probably the male, which ejects the young from the nest soon after they hatch. It is all too common an occurrence (see Chapter 4). The explanation for this curious behaviour appears to be that the male gets out of phase with the female in the breeding cycle. It should be a co-operative venture and male and female should both be in the nestling-rearing phase when the eggs hatch. Evidently the male reverts to the courtship stage and is intent on starting the cycle again. A similar explanation probably holds true for the habit of building 'egg sandwiches', which is said to be common in the Zebra Finch and occasionally occurs in the Gouldian Finch. One or both members of the pair revert to the nest-building phase after egg-laying, and a new nest is constructed on top of the existing eggs. Possible causes and solutions to these problems are as follows.

1) The birds may be under stress (see above). One method of increasing their security is to cover half of the front of the cage with brown paper. Nest box inspection should be cut out altogether.

2) The birds may be over-stimulated by taking too much of their enriched diet. Leave soft food out of it temporarily, until just before the eggs are due to hatch.

Nestlings dead in shell

A small number of deaths of embryos within the eggs is probably inevitable but excessive mortality should be explored further. There are four principal causes. First, it may be the result of loss of too much water by evaporation, caused by the air in the birdroom being too dry (see Chapter 5). Second, it may

80

be due to deficiency of a particular nutrient, such as a vitamin or more often a mineral. Third, it may be caused by a bacteria infection, such as *Salmonella*. Fourth, the strain may have poor hatchability.

The crops of nestlings have air in them

This is normal and is no cause for concern.

The nestlings' skin is dull and wrinkled

This is a symptom of inadequate feeding by the parents. The possibility that they are neglecting their broods can be confirmed by checking that the nestlings' crops are full in the evenings. If they are not, the condition of the parents themselves should be explored. They may be suffering from intestinal problems, which are indicated by soiled vents. An alternative possibility is that the parents are feeding hard seed to their young before they can digest it properly; their droppings then become a beige/oatmeal colour. The solution in this case is to remove the dry seed mix from the cage and provide only soft food and soaked seed.

Nestling diarrhoea

Their droppings become watery, and probably white, and the whole nest box is wet and messy. The feathers of the brood and parents become soiled. It is necessary to change the nest, removing the soiled material and replacing it with clean grass or fibre. Antibiotics should be administered to the drinking water (see Chapter 14).

Canker

The tiny protozoan parasite *Trichomonas* is sometimes the cause of nestlings' deaths. It occurs in the mouth and produces white, cotton wool or cream-like patches, which can be seen when the nestling gapes for food. The first symptoms are likely to appear in nestlings aged about five days or older. They are usually weak and listless and their crops may be empty. It is wise to cull them since they are unlikely to survive and are an obvious source of further infection.

Hand-feeding neglected young

Occasionally a pair of rearing adults will go out of condition and will neglect or even desert their nestlings. They should be fostered to other parents (assuming that some are available) but hand-feeding will increase their chances of surviving. This can be done with a specially-manufactured hand-feeding syringe or by fitting commercially available crop needles on to an ordinary hypodermic syringe. The food supplied must be semi-liquid, and the following formula is recommended.

One teaspoon of powdered milk protein

Two teaspoons of plain flour

0.2g of one of the antibiotics aureomycin or terramycin

Half a teaspoon of multi-vitamin/mineral supplement

This is mixed to the consistency of thick double (heavy) cream by adding boiling water.

The food is poured into the syringe while it is still warm and fed to the chick when it is of about body temperature. Before doing this, air is expelled from it. The syringe is held vertically and tapped so that the air bubbles are driven to the top, and the plunger is depressed gently until they are expelled. The nest box containing the nestlings is placed on a convenient table or bench and its lid is removed. This movement usually stimulates the chicks to gape and, if this fails, they will probably respond to slight rocking of the nest box. The hand, which is holding the syringe, should be steadied by resting it on the side of the nest box, and the feeding needle inserted into the gaping mouth of one of the nestlings. It is then pushed slowly into the crop. The chick will assist by swallowing. The plunger is depressed gradually filling the crop with food and the needle is withdrawn as this happens, taking care to stop the procedure before food overflows into the mouth. Any excess which does so is carefully removed with a matchstick, since it might cause the nestling to choke. Excess is similarly removed from the beak. Hand-feeding must be repeated every two hours until the parents take over the duty.

Nestlings which are taken from the nest must be kept at a temperature of about 35°C (95°F). They should be fed every two hours, with no longer than a five-hour gap at night.

9 COLONY BREEDING

Although cage breeding is generally believed to be the most efficient way of propagating Gouldian Finches, it is not everyone's wish to breed them in this way. There are many aviculturists who prefer to give the species the full opportunity of displaying its magnificent colouration by keeping and breeding it in large flights. It looks particularly attractive in outdoor flights. Indeed, there can be few more beautiful sights than that of a colony of Gouldian Finches, of mixed head colours, living in a well-planted aviary. The main objective of this chapter is to consider the problems of colony breeding, paying special attention to their needs out-of-doors, where they must cope with the vagaries of the local climate. Nevertheless, much of what is written applies equally well to the upkeep of colonies in indoor flights.

It is no coincidence that this chapter is much shorter than that which deals with cage breeding. Colony breeding is, to a degree, a matter of allowing the birds to get on with things for themselves. They are allowed to select their own mates and are generally spared intrusions, such as those of regular nest box inspections. They will reward you by showing their full range of behaviour in the aviary and dispel forever the myth that the Gouldian Finch is an inactive creature. Nothing could be further from the truth. When given the opportunity, it is as lively and entertaining as most of the other small finches.

HARDINESS

Aviculturists who have the advantage of an agreeable climate for much of the year, such as in Australia, South Africa and southern parts of the United States, commonly breed their birds in colonies in outside flights. Surprisingly, in view of the Gouldian Finch's reputation as a delicate species, it is sometimes kept and bred out-of-doors in northern Europe. As mentioned in Chapter 4, acclimatised birds show a remarkable ability to tolerate cold, and Teague, for example, kept his birds in unheated quarters throughout English winters. Climate is nevertheless an important factor and Mr W. Bain (*Australian Aviculture*, May 1959, pp. 79–80) wrote as follows of his difficulties of breeding them in outdoor aviaries in Scotland:

Gouldians placed in garden aviaries are reluctant to roost in the shelter provided, with the result that they may get chills which invariably turn to pneumonia with fatal results. The most successful aviaries for breeding Gouldians are the box pattern type, all closed except the front which should have Windowlite shutters which can be adjusted during inclement weather.

Mr Bain had some success, however, and his frustrations should perhaps be heralded as a warning for caution, rather than one never to try the Gouldian Finch out-of-doors. Mr Rae V. Anderson of California redresses the balance of opinion in an article in *Foreign Birds* which was subsequently reprinted in *The Grassfinch* (1984, Vol. 8, pp. 25–36). He is emphatic in his claim that properly acclimatised birds are hardy:

Even though I live in Southern California quite close to our border with Mexico, we are in a valley and far enough inland to have fairly substantial extremes in temperature. Winter temperatures this year have dropped to 16°F (−9°C) on successive nights. In every case however the temperature here rose again by noon to above freezing. In a flock of well over one hundred not one Gouldian has been lost during these cold spells. Large water dishes were completely frozen and supplemental water had to be put in the cages each morning until the weather warmed. In summer the majority of our days are in the 90s°F with a few to 105°F and an occasional 115°F. I have not yet lost a Gouldian during or shortly after these extremes.

My aviaries are largely open, four to six feet of the top being covered at each end. The back is covered from roof to the ground. Four feet of the side adjacent to the back of the cages at the extreme ends of the battery of aviaries is also covered. The shelter is actually part of the flight with no doors, partitions or curtains of any kind to close it off or separate it from the flight. Otherwise sides and top are aviary wire with no other protection. I offer them only enough protection to keep the rain and dew off them if they elect to use the shelter and to prevent the wind from blasting completely unimpeded through the shelter area. Although these birds are hardy, I am not at all sure that they would survive temperatures near 0°F without some form of additional protection. You can however make hothouse creatures of them by pampering.

Most, if not all, writers are in full agreement, however, that Gouldian Finches are delicate when first introduced into outdoor flights and are always susceptible to draughts. It is necessary therefore to protect flights from exposure to chilling winds, possibly even by covering them on three sides. In northern Europe, and areas of similar climate, where the weather is often cold, damp and windy for long periods, it is strongly desirable to give the birds access to a heated shelter. They can be acclimatised to life out-of-doors by releasing them into flights during spells of warm weather in late spring or summer, keeping them under close watch for signs of illness.

BREEDING

Birds must not be over-crowded. No more than three or four pairs should be housed in a flight, which has an outside section measuring 3.7×1.2×1.8m high (12×4×6ft) and an indoor one measuring 1.2×0.9×1.8m (4×3×6ft). Obviously larger numbers can be accommodated as the size of the flights is increased. Other species of birds may interfere with attempts of the Gouldian Finches to breed by, for example, competing with them for nest sites and nesting materials. It is therefore wise to exclude them altogether.

Attention to diet is as important for birds which are breeding in colonies as for those in cages and it is recommended that feeding follows the schedule outlined in Chapter 7. The relatively austere diet during the non-breeding season is followed by an enriched one, which includes soft food, soaked seed and/or seeding grasses, during the breeding season. The change to this protein-rich diet should bring the birds into breeding condition, and this process will be accelerated by the provision of nest boxes in the aviary. It is necessary to supply abundant nest boxes, probably at least two per pair of birds. They should be well spaced out but leaving an area in the flight which is entirely free from them. The birds will use it as a place for daily social gathering. This is characteristic of the behaviour of wild birds during the breeding season (see Chapter 3) and, given sufficient space, is also performed by captive ones.

Breeding is restricted to the summer when the birds have the benefit of long hours of daylight in which to rear their young. They shuld be allowed to rear no more than two or three broods and nest boxes are, in any case, removed as the autumn approaches. The frustrations of permitting the birds to breed late in the season are well illustrated by the experiences of Mr G. Bailey *(The Grassfinch,* 1984, Vol. 8, pp. 37–39). A pair of his birds nested in an outdoor flight in England during a cold, damp week late in October. All four eggs in the clutch hatched in mid-November and the young nestlings survived a period of extremely cold weather with temperatures well below 0°C (32°F). Drinking water was invariably frozen overnight. The female rarely left the nest during the daytime, presumably to keep the nestlings warm, and also roosted in it for at least the first 10 days. Late in November the young died over a four-day period. They were small and thin, and Mr Bailey suggests that this was largely because the short period of daylight (approximately 7 hours) was too short for the parents to provide sufficient food for them.

PROWLERS

One of the problems of outside aviaries is that they attract the attention of potential predators. Rats will burrow into flights if they are given the chance and, since they will kill the birds, must be excluded (see Chapter 5). Cats are also a hazard because, even though they cannot get into the flight, they will lunge at the birds within it. The panic-stricken attempts to escape by the inhabitants sometimes results in them seriously injuring themselves. Furthermore, the presence of a cat totally disrupts the normal routine in the flight and this can cause breeding failures. Natural predators including predatory birds and, in some countries, snakes may cause similar problems. One solution is to build a false wire netting roof about 30cm (1ft) above the existing roof of the aviary, and where extreme problems are encountered on the side also. This 'distances' the predators from the aviary's inhabitants and may deter them from attacking altogether. Wire should of course be sunk into the ground in order to exclude burrowing predators.

HARDY STRAINS

Mr G. Bailey (see above) argues persuasively for the need to produce Gouldian Finches which can survive even in temperate climates without the provision of additional heat. He suggests that this will never be possible as long as we attempt to re-create the climate of northern Australia within our birdrooms. The answer must surely be for enthusiasts to develop hardy aviary bred strains by line-breeding (see Chapter 12). It may seem undesirable to aim for separate 'birdroom' and 'aviary-bred' varieties of the Gouldian Finch, but, at present, this is probably the only practical solution. One day all Gouldian Finches may be as hardy and prolific as the Zebra Finch, but in the meantime it is unrealistic to expect the breeder who is, for example attempting to establish a new mutation in his birdroom, to risk his stock by transferring it to unheated aviaries.

10 BENGALESE FINCHES AS FOSTER PARENTS

The potential dangers of rearing Gouldian Finches under Bengalese Finch foster parents have already been stressed in Chapter 4 and, in general, we do not advocate this method. There are, nevertheless, situations, such as in establishing a new mutation (see Chapter 13) or producing large numbers of young in order to select strongly for a desirable character, in which we believe that its use is justifiable. The first part of this chapter describes therefore the method of foster-rearing, although we strongly recommend that those who do use it will at the very least introduce safeguards to ensure that they do not create strains of Gouldian Finches which cannot rear their own young. This can be done by foster-rearing young only from parents which have already demonstrated that they have the ability to self-rear. A highly-recommended procedure is to alternate broods between the two methods: the first brood is foster-reared, the second is reared by the natural parents, and so on.

The second part of the chapter deals with the problem of imprinting, and also describes the process of song learning. Imprinting is a much debated subject by breeders of Australian Finches because of the fear that birds which have imprinted on foster parents will not mate with members of their own species when they reach sexual maturity. Scientific research on this topic has been carried out on various species and it is necessary therefore to refer to the results of experiments on the Greylag Goose and the Zebra Finch before discussing the problem in the Gouldian Finch itself.

CATERING FOR THE BENGALESE FINCH

The first need is to obtain good birds. Some strains of Bengalese Finches are much more willing to foster-rear than others, and care in locating a reliable strain will be well-rewarded. The next essential is to ensure that the birds which are to be used as foster parents are in first-rate condition. Too many breeders treat their Bengalese Finches as second-class citizens and then wonder why they get second-class results! The culture of this bird is dealt with in a book by Mr James Buchan (*The Bengalese Finch*, 1976, published by Isles d'Avon Ltd, Bristol) but, fortunately for the Gouldian Finch breeder, it lives extremely well if it is given almost identical treatment to that of the Gouldian

Finch. This includes the annual diet and breeding schedules (Chapter 7 and 8). The Bengalese Finches are allowed to fly in outside flights during the non-breeding period and are provided with the austere diet based on dry seed. They are then brought back into the birdroom for breeding at the same time as the Gouldian Finch, and stimulated to come into breeding condition by supplying them with protein-rich foods. They are catholic in their eating habits and readily take soft foods provided for them, even if they are not familiar with them.

SEXING BIRDS

One problem presented by the Bengalese Finch, which we do not have with the Gouldian Finch, is in sexing birds: there are no obvious differences between male and female Bengalese Finches. The male can, however, be identified by its courtship display, during the performance of which he fluffs out his feathers and 'bounces' along the perch towards another bird, continuously singing an unmelodious song as he does so. A bird which performs this display is certainly a male but it cannot be assumed that the object of his affections is a female. Male Bengalese Finches seem to have almost as much difficulty in recognising females of the species as we do. They are highly likely to court males, particularly on first introduction to them.

A common way of sexing youngsters is to isolate them individually in cages which are divided into sections by wooden partitions. After a day or so in isolation, birds in adjacent cages are introduced to one another by removing the partition between them. Those which display are immediately identified as males but birds which fail to display are tested again on the following day, and, if they are still unresponsive, are assumed to be females. Sexed birds can be colour-ringed appropriately, using blue rings for the males and pink ones for the females, and giving each bird a second colour ring to indicate the year of its birth. Subsequent pairings will confirm the sex identification for true male-female pairs will produce fertile clutches of 4 to 6 eggs. Male-male 'pairs' will obviously not produce any eggs at all, whereas female-female pairs are likely to produce an abundance of them, often at the rate of two per day. These abnormal 'pairs' will however incubate eggs of other birds and will often rear the young. They are, nevertheless, generally less reliable than true pairs in so doing and it is therefore well worth taking the extra trouble to sex birds accurately.

BREEDING CAGES

Cages no bigger than 38×30×38cm high (15×12×15in) are suitable for breeding Bengalese Finches and, indeed, many breeders find that they perform their duties more successfully in small cages than in large ones. They suggest that this is because the parents are always in close proximity to the chicks, and are therefore more responsive to their begging calls. Cages can be constructed from the traditional materials and many breeders use those of box-type design with wire fronts, but all wire cages, which can be constructed from welded wire mesh (16 gauge), have proved to be particularly effective. The sides, roof and floor are cut to the required dimensions and then joined together with 'C' clips (or similar means). The cages should be serviced from outside so that openings must be made in the front for access doors, feeding and watering utensils and nest boxes. The doors themselves can be hinged squares of netting, each of which is larger than the opening. Nest boxes are the usual half open type.

FOSTERING

It is wise to set up more pairs of Bengalese Finches (probably twice as many) than are needed for fostering, thereby ensuring that there are enough in the correct phase of nesting to receive the Gouldian Finch eggs. Clutches of eggs are removed from their natural Gouldian Finch parents when they are complete and transferred to Bengalese Finches which have themselves just started to incubate at about their third or fourth egg. It is inadvisable to rear mixed broods of different species since the parents tend to neglect the fostered young, and it is necessary therefore to remove the Bengalese Finches' own eggs, together with any that are laid after the transfer. In order to recognise the Gouldian Finch eggs and distinguish them from any newly-laid ones, each is marked with a felt-tipped pen. Bengalese Finches are extraordinarily adaptable parents, and eggs, or even young, can be transferred to them at other stages in the nesting cycle, although with varying degrees of success. The introduction of small nestlings into broods of larger ones is normally unsuccessful, however, because they must compete with nest mates for their parents' attentions, and may receive insufficient food to survive.

The feeding procedure is exactly the same as that described in Chapters 7 and 8 for Gouldian Finches which are rearing their own young. Bengalese Finches are attentive parents and are extremely tolerant of nest box inspections. The young develop as rapidly as they do with normal parents, they fledge at the usual age (see Chapter 8), and can be removed from their parents at 35 days of age. Treatment is then the same as that for any other juvenile Gouldian Finches (see Chapter 8).

Thought must be given to breeding some Bengalese Finches in order to provide sufficient birds for the following years' fostering requirements. It is recommended that this is done by transferring eggs from the Bengalese Finches which have proved to be the best foster parents to pairs which have been less successful, and allow the latter to foster the young. In this way, the maximum use is made of the best foster parents in raising Gouldian Finches but their young (with luck inheriting their 'good' traits) are also reared for the next generation.

THE PROBLEM OF IMPRINTING

The process of imprinting was brought to the attention of the scientific world by the famous Austrian biologist, Professor Konrad Lorenz. He showed that goslings of the Greylag Goose became attached to (imprinted on) a mother figure soon after hatching, and thereafter followed her and ran to her whenever danger threatened. Goslings normally imprint on their natural mother but Lorenz showed that, if the natural mother is not present, they will imprint on other objects, even human beings. He divided one clutch of goose eggs into two, allowing one group to be incubated and hatched by the mother, but the other group to be raised in an incubator. The goslings hatched by the mother imprinted on her and followed her but those hatched in the incubator imprinted on Lorenz. They treated him as the mother, following him wherever he went. They even did so when they were given a choice between following Lorenz and their true mother.

Imprinting of young on parents, so-called filial imprinting, is important in keeping the family group together, but the process can also have profound effects on the behaviour of an individual when it becomes adult. This is the case in sexual imprinting. The developing individual sexually imprints on its parents and, on becoming mature, will pair only with a member of that species. This phenomenon normally goes unnoticed because young are reared by, and imprint on, their natural parents, so that subsequently they mate with one of their own kind. The problem arises when foster-rearing techniques are used. Professor Klaus Immelmann (*Proceedings of the XVth International Ornithological Congress*, 1972, pp. 316–338) showed that male Zebra Finches which were reared under Bengalese Finches imprinted on their foster parents, and behaved, on reaching maturity, as if they were Bengalese Finches. This was clearly demonstrated in tests in which each of several foster-reared males was given the opportunity to court either a female Zebra Finch or a female Bengalese Finch. Almost all of them directed their displays to the Bengalese Finch even though she was totally unreceptive. The female Zebra Finch often solicited attention from the males but she was usually ignored.

The imprinting process tends to be irreversible. Immelmann discovered that this was the case in foster-reared male Zebra Finches, even after they had been persuaded to breed with female Zebra Finches. They would eventually do so if they were caged with them in isolation of Bengalese Finches but their breeding experience did not destroy the original effects of imprinting. These males still preferred to court female Bengalese Finches rather than unfamiliar female Zebra Finches in choice tests.

SONG LEARNING

Song in many birds, including the Zebra Finch, is largely acquired by learning during the animal's early life. A simple song is inborn (i.e. it is already programmed within the nervous system) because hand-reared young male Zebra Finches, which are kept in sound-proof boxes so that they cannot hear other Zebra Finches singing, still sing on reaching maturity. Their songs, however, contain fewer elements than normal songs and are relatively slow in tempo. The full song is only acquired by males which have the chance of listening to other males singing. They copy their songs. This learning occurs, however, in young birds and most of them learn to copy their father's song. Remarkably, those which are foster-reared learn to sing the song of the Bengalese Finch foster father, rather than that of a Zebra Finch, and sound like Bengalese Finches when they sing as adults.

IMPRINTING AND SONG LEARNING IN THE GOULDIAN FINCH

There is unfortunately relatively little information on the effects of early experience on the behaviour of the Gouldian Finch.

There is some evidence that male Gouldian Finches learn their songs from other birds and, in some cases in captivity, may learn the song of the wrong species. Dr Luis Baptista (*Auk*, 1973, Vol. 90, pp. 891–894) describes a case in which one male, which had been reared by Bengalese Finches, was, at the age of about a month, released into a cage containing a pair of Red Avadavats,

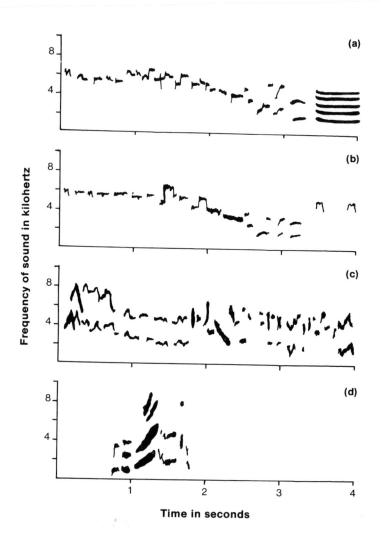

Fig. 19 *Drawings of the sonagrams (sound spectrographs) of: (a) the song of a Red Avadavat; (b) the song of a Gouldian Finch which was kept with Avadavats; (c) a more typical Gouldian Finch song; and (d) a Bengalese Finch song. (a) and (b) are based on a figure in a paper by L. Baptista (Auk, 1973, Vol. 90, pp 891–894).*

together with Bengalese and Gouldian Finches. It learned its song from the male Avadavat. This was given in the typical whispering way of the Gouldian Finch but comparisons of the sound spectrograms leave no doubt that it was a version of the Avadavat's song (Fig. 19).

The particular fear that foster-reared Gouldian Finches will not pair with members of their own species, as a result of the effects of imprinting, is however unfounded. It is common experience that Gouldian Finches which have been raised by Bengalese will pair with their own kind, and make good parents. The explanation may be that, like foster-reared Zebra Finches (see above), fostered Gouldian Finches will pair together but only when there are no Bengalese Finches available as potential mates. The whole subject is clearly an open one and in need of further research.

11 GENETICS

There are, in addition to the three naturally-occuring head-colour varieties of the Gouldian Finch, several domestic mutations (see Chapter 13). Some breeders are happy enough to allow different varieties to interbreed haphazardly but others prefer to control matings between their birds, and be in a position to predict their outcome. This becomes particularly important when attempts are being made to breed pure strains or to establish new mutations. Unfortunately, predicting the outcomes of matings requires a knowledge and understanding of genetics, and it may not be everyone's wish to fathom the mysteries of this difficult science. We have therefore tried to cater for all needs in this chapter. We have done so by giving an introductory account of the ways in which characters, such as those determining breast and head colours, are transmitted from one generation of Gouldian Finches to the next. We have also provided details of mating expectations which can be used without an understanding of the underlying principles of genetics.

The inheritance of head colours in the Gouldian Finch is more complex than that concerned with colour mutations in many other domestic birds. Dr H. N. Southern, a research biologist, used the breeding results of Mr P. W. Teague and others to work out the genetics of red-headedness/black-headedness (*Journal of Genetics,* 1945, Vol. 46, pp. 51–57). Later Mr Ray Murray (*Avicultural Magazine,* 1963, Vol. 69, pp. 108–113) determined the inheritance of yellow-headedness from his own breeding experiments in Melbourne. More recently, Mr F. Barnicoat (*Australian Aviculture,* April 1967, pp. 49–50) succeeded not only in establishing the white-breasted mutation in South Africa but also in showing how this character is inherited from one generation to the next.

CHROMOSOMES

Each bird starts its life as a single cell, the fertilised egg. This divides into two cells, then by repeated divisions into four, eight, sixteen, thirty-two, continuing until it becomes the millions of cells which make up the whole organism. Development is remarkably precise, however, so that the fertilised Gouldian Finch egg is programmed to become an adult of that species, a fertilised Zebra Finch egg develops into an adult Zebra Finch, and so on. Clearly, there must be a set of instructions, or blueprint, within the fertilised egg which determines the exact pattern of development. Furthermore, since each animal develops some of its father's characters and also some of its mother's, the blueprint must be derived in part from both parents.

The instructions for development are, in fact, contained within the part of the cell which is known as the nucleus (Fig. 20). It contains several pairs of

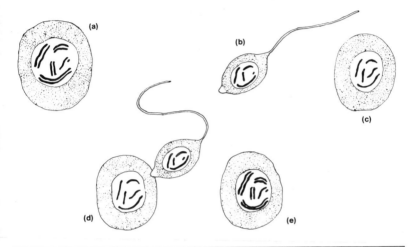

Fig. 20 *Highly diagrammatic drawings of cells. (a) A cell whose nucleus has a full complement (two sets) of chromosomes; (b) and (c) a sperm and an egg whose nuclei each have only one set of chromosomes; (d) a sperm in the process of fertilising (fusing with) an egg; and (e) the fertilised egg which now has the full complement of chromosomes.*

thread-like structures, the chromosomes. Most cells of the body contain two complete sets of them (i.e. they occur in pairs) but the germ cells, the sperms and eggs, contain only one full set (i.e. half the number of chromosomes of the other cells). This is important because, when fertilisation occurs, the sperm's nucleus fuses with that of the egg, and the fertilised egg then has two sets of chromosomes: one from the father and one from the mother.

HEREDITARY FACTORS AND MATING EXPECTATIONS

The actual units of inheritance, or hereditary factors, are carried on the chromosomes. Since each ordinary cell of the body has two sets of chromosomes, it follows that there are two (or multiples of two) hereditary factors controlling each character. Let us consider the inheritance of breast colour in the Gouldian Finch. This can either be purple, as in wild birds and most domestic ones, or white, as in the white-breasted mutation. There is therefore a factor for normal purple-breastedness, which we shall refer to as P, and one for white-breastedness, which we shall symbolise as p. In most normal birds both factors will be P; they can be expressed symbolically as PP. White-breasted birds are pp. There is a third possibility, however. Some birds may be 'mixed' for these factors, carrying one P factor and one p factor: they are Pp. P is dominant to p (which is said to be recessive) and such a bird will have a normal, purple breast. Since it carries an unexpressed factor for white-breastedness it is often called a split or, more fully, a normal split for the white-breasted factor.

We are now in a position to consider some matings between birds. Suppose we cross a normal male *(PP)* with a white-breasted female *(pp)*:

	male		female
Parents	*PP*	×	*pp*

Each of the germ cells of these two birds will contain only one of the pair of factors:

	male		female
Parents	*PP*	×	*pp*
Germ cells	*P* *P*		*p* *p*
	sperms		eggs

The fusion of sperm and egg at fertilisation restores the double set of chromosomes in the embryo, and it will have two factors for this breast colouration, one from each parent:

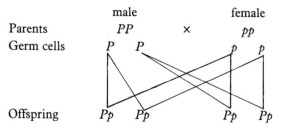

All offspring from this particular mating will therefore be the same as far as breast colouration is concerned. They will be normal in appearance but split for the white-breasted factor *(Pp)*.

Different mating expectations are obtained if we cross two of these splits *(Pp)* together:

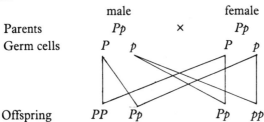

	male		female
Parents	*Pp*	×	*Pp*
Germ cells	*P* *p*		*P* *p*
Offspring	*PP* *Pp*		*Pp* *pp*

The result is that young will be produced in the ratio of 3 with normal purple breasts to 1 white-breasted individual, or, more accurately, 1 normal *(PP)*: 2 splits *(Pp)*: 1 white-breasted *(pp)*.

Other possible matings are worked out in exactly the same way, and their expectations are presented on p. 103. It should be stressed, however, that, although actual breeding results are likely to be close to theoretical predictions, particularly when large numbers of young are involved, they may not be exactly the same as them. The precise numbers depend on chance and it would be quite possible to get two or more white-breasted individuals in some broods of young from this mating, but others with none at all. (See, for example, the results of Mr Barnicoat's first matings when he was establishing this mutation; Chapter 13.)

SEX DETERMINATION AND SEX LINKAGE

The sex of an individual is determined by one pair of chromosomes, the sex chromosomes. This pair is unlike other (so-called autosomal) pairs of chromosomes in the female. One of them, the *Y* chromosome, is short and almost vestigial in structure; the other sex chromosome, the *X* chromosome, is much like any other chromosome in appearance. The sex chromosomes of males are both *X*. All females are therefore *XY* and all males are *XX*. This arrangement ensures that equal numbers of males and females are produced in the population. All of the male's sperms carry a single *X* chromosome but the female's eggs are of two kinds: half carry an *X* chromosome and half a *Y* chromosome. Mating expectations, with regard to the sex of offspring, are always therefore as follows:

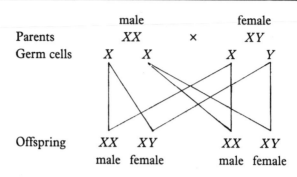

	male		female
Parents	XX	×	XY
Germ cells	X X		X Y

Offspring	XX XY		XX XY
	male female		male female

In other words, half of the young should be males and half females. (Mammals are incidentally different from birds with regard to their sex chromosomes: male mammals are XY and females are XX.)

Hereditary factors which are sited on the sex chromosomes are said to be sex-linked. Their inheritance from one generation to the next does not follow the same rules as those described above for factors which are carried on pairs of autosomal chromosomes. This is because the vestigial Y chromosome does not carry factors. The female therefore has only one set of sex-linked factors: those on her X chromosome.

The male has two sets of factors. This can be understood by considering the pair of sex-linked factors which control red-headedness/black-headedness in the Gouldian Finch. The factor for red-headedness, R, is dominant to that for black-headedness, r. The possible combinations of these factors in birds are therefore as follows:

Sex	Sex chromosomes	Factors carried	Head colour
male	XX	RR	red
	XX	Rr	red (split black)
	XX	rr	black
female	XY	RO	red
	XY	rO	black

The symbol O indicates the absence of the second factor on the Y chromosome. It can be seen that a single dose of a recessive factor can express itself in the female: rO results in black-headedness. Unlike males, females cannot be split for a sex-linked factor.

There are six possible matings between these birds.

Mating 1

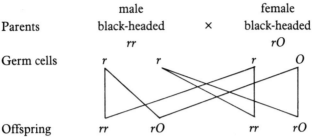

This mating is straightforward. The offspring are always the same as the parents: they are all black-headed.

Mating 2

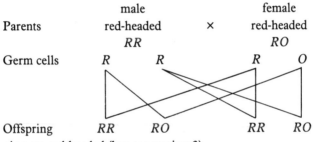

All offspring are red-headed (but see mating 3).

Mating 3

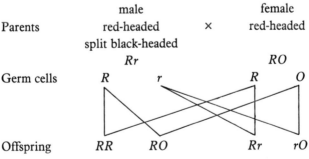

In this case, all of the male offspring will be red-headed but half of them will be split for black-headed. Half of the females will be red and half black.

Mating 4

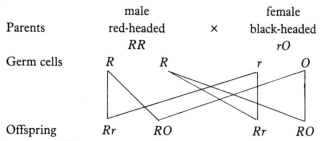

	male			female	
Parents	red-headed		×	black-headed	
	RR			rO	
Germ cells	R	R		r	O
Offspring	Rr	RO		Rr	RO

All of the young will be red-headed but the males will be split for black-headedness.

Mating 5

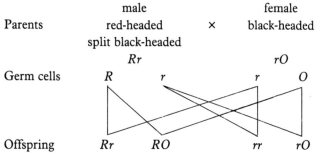

	male			female	
Parents	red-headed		×	black-headed	
	split black-headed				
	Rr			rO	
Germ cells	R	r		r	O
Offspring	Rr	RO		rr	rO

Half the young will be black and half red, but the male red-heads will be split for black.

Mating 6

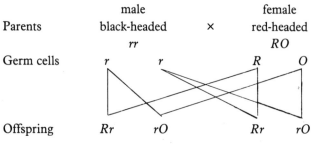

	male			female	
Parents	black-headed		×	red-headed	
	rr			RO	
Germ cells	r	r		R	O
Offspring	Rr	rO		Rr	rO

Whereas the father is black his sons will be red (split black); and whereas the mother is red, her daughters will be black.

Dr Southern found that these theoretical breeding expectations were borne out by the actual results of aviculturists (Table 13), verifying that the factors are indeed sex-linked ones. They evidently act on the mechanism for manufacturing the black pigment eumelanin in the head feathers: r stimulates its production; R inhibits it.

TABLE 13
The numbers of black-headed and red-headed young, predicted on the basis that black/red head colour is determined by a pair of sex-linked factors, and those actually obtained from matings between birds. Detailed records were kept of five of the six possible matings (see text). Records were not made for mating number 1, which was carried out many times, always with the same result. Information from H.N. Southern *(Journal of Genetics, 1945, Vol. 46, pp. 51–57).*

Mating Number	Pair male	female	Total number of young		Numbers of young Males Red	Black	Females Red	Black
1	Black (rr)	Black (rO)		predicted actual	– –	100% 100%	– –	100% 100%
2	Red (RR)	Red (RO)	28	predicted actual	14 13	0 0	14 15	0 0
3	Red (Rr)	Red (RO)	35	predicted actual	17.5 15	0 0	8.75 6	8.75 14
4	Red (RR)	Black (rO)	12	predicted actual	3 3	3 2	3 4	3 3
5	Red (Rr)	Black (rO)	12	predicted actual	6 9	0 0	6 3	0 0
6	Black (rr)	Red (RO)	31	predicted actual	15.5 12	0 0	0 0	15.5 19

YELLOW-HEADEDNESS

So far we have ignored the fact that Gouldian Finches can be yellow-headed. In fact, this character is determined by factors which operate on the mechanism whereby the yellow pigment lutein is converted to the red one, astaxantin (see Chapter 1). They are carried on autosomal chromosomes so that their inheritance shows the same rules as those described for breast colouration. There is a dominant factor Y in whose presence lutein is converted to astaxantin. The recessive factor y inhibits this conversion. Thus, birds which are either YY or Yy have astaxantin in their head feathers and are therefore potentially red-headed; those which are yy have lutein in the head feathers and are therefore potentially yellow-headed.

Most Gouldian Finches carry more than one colour pigment in the head feathers, and the actual head colour depends on the combined effects of the two mechanisms controlling the manufacture of eumelanin and astaxantin. Birds which possess eumelanin will have in addition either astaxantin or lutein but they will be black-headed because eumelanin masks the effect of these other pigments. Birds which lack eumelanin will be either red-headed or yellow-headed, depending on whether they possess astaxantin or lutein in the head feathers.

There are 15 possible combinations of these two pairs of factors, although several of them result in the same visual effect (Table 14). For instance, $rrYY$,

TABLE 14
Possible combinations of the pairs of factors controlling red/black head colour and red/yellow head colour, and their effects on head and beak colouration.

Sex	Factors controlling red/black head colour	red/yellow head colour	Actual head colouration	Beak colouration
Males	RR	YY	Red	Red
	RR	Yy	Red	Red
	RR	yy	Yellow	Yellow
	Rr	YY	Red	Red
	Rr	Yy	Red	Red
	Rr	yy	Yellow	Yellow
	rr	YY	Black	Red
	rr	Yy	Black	Red
	rr	yy	Black	Yellow
Females	RO	YY	Red	Red
	RO	Yy	Red	Red
	RO	yy	Yellow	Yellow
	rO	YY	Black	Red
	rO	Yy	Black	Red
	rO	yy	Black	Yellow

rrYy and *rryy* are all black-headed males. Strictly, they are black-headed/red-headed, black-headed/red-headed and black-headed/yellow-headed respectively.

In some cases, it is possible to gain further information about the factors which are being carried by looking at beak colour. This is because astaxantin or lutein is produced in the tip of the beak and this is under the control of the same factors which control their manufacture in the head feathers. Beak colour is not, however, masked by eumelanin, even in black-headed birds. It follows that a black-headed bird which is *rryy* will have a yellow-tipped (lutein) beak; those which are *rrYY* and *rrYy* will have red-tipped (astaxantin) beaks.

It is of course possible to mate any of the nine males shown in Table 14 with any of the six females. There are therefore 54 possible matings between them. The expectations from these are shown on pp. 104–111. Mr Ray Murray unravelled the inheritance of yellow-headedness/red-headedness by considering eight of these. Again, he compared the numbers of young of different head colours actually produced from these matings with those expected on theoretical grounds. The close fits between the two sets of figures (see Table 15) confirms the hypothesis; yellow-headedness/red-headedness is determined by a single pair of factors which are carried on autosomal chromosomes.

MATING EXPECTATIONS FOR WHITE-BREASTEDNESS

There are six possible matings. Abbreviations used to describe them are as follows: N = normal (purple) breast; W = white-breast; NW = normal split for white-breasted. Note that proportions of offsprings are expressed in percentages.

Mating No.	Parents			Offspring (per cent)
1	N *(PP)*	×	N *(PP)*	100 N *(PP)*
2	W *(pp)*	×	W *(pp)*	100 W *(pp)*
3	N *(PP)*	×	W *(pp)*	100 NW *(Pp)*
4	NW *(Pp)*	×	NW *(Pp)*	25 N *(PP)*; 50 NW *(Pp)*; 25 W *(pp)*
5	NW *(Pp)*	×	W *(pp)*	50 NW *(Pp)*; 50 W *(pp)*
6	NW *(Pp)*	×	N *(PP)*	50 N *(PP)*; 50 NW *(Pp)*

TABLE 15

The predicted results of eight matings between birds of different head colours on the basis that red/yellow head colour is determined by a single pair of factors (carried on autosomal chromosomes), compared with those obtained by actually breeding birds. The experiments were carried out by Mr R. Murray *(Avicultural Magazine,* 1963, Vol. 69, pp. 108–113).

Mating Number	Pair Male	Female	Total number young recorded	
1	Yellow	Black	19	predicted
	(RRyy)	*(rOYY)*		actual
2	Red	Red	52	predicted
	(RrYy)	*(ROYy)*		actual
3	Red	Black	9	predicted
	(RrYy)	*(rOYy)*		actual
4	Yellow	Yellow	14	predicted
	(Rryy)	*(ROyy)*		actual
5	Yellow	Black	13	predicted
	(Rryy)	*(rOYy)*		actual
6	Black	Yellow	4	predicted
	(rrYY)	*(ROyy)*		actual
7	Black	Black	17	predicted
	(rryy)	*(rOyy)*		actual
8	Black	Yellow	9	predicted
	(rryy)	*(ROyy)*		actual

MATING EXPECTATIONS FOR HEAD COLOUR

There are 15 possible combinations of the two pairs of factors which determine head colour: 9 possible males and 6 females (see Table 14). One pair of these factors is sex-linked and the other is carried on autosomal chromosomes and consequently the procedure for calculating the expected offspring from any particular mating is complex. It is done by working out the factors which will be carried by germ cells from each parent and then working out the result of fusions (fertilisations) between them. An example will help to make it clearer.

	Males			Females	
		Numbers of young			
Yellow	Red	Black	Yellow	Red	Black
0	12	0	0	7	0
0	12	0	0	7	0
5.3	16.8	0	11.6	3.9	15.5
5	16	0	2	9	20
0.5	1.5	2	0.6	1.9	2.5
1	1	2	1	2	2
6	0	0	4	0	4
6	0	0	3	0	5
1.8	1.8	3.5	1.5	1.5	3
1	3	3	2	2	2
0	1	0	0	0	3
0	1	0	0	0	3
0	0	7	0	0	10
0	0	7	0	0	10
4	0	0	0	0	5
4	0	0	0	0	5

Suppose we cross a Red-headed male $(RrYy)$ with a Black-headed female $(rOYy)$. Each will produce four kinds of germ cells as follows:

Parents	Red-headed male	×	Black-headed female
	$(RrYy)$		$(rOYy)$

Germ cells RY Ry rY ry rY ry OY Oy

Each of the four kinds of germ cell produced by one parent can fuse with any one of those of the other parent so that there were 16 (4×4) different possibilities. These are most easily scored by casting them in a matrix of the kind illustrated in Table 16. It can be seen that three head colours appear in the offspring, which are as follows:

Males:

	3 Red-headed	*(RrYY; RrYy; RrYy)*
	4 Black-headed	*(rrYY; rrYy; rrYy; rryy)*
	1 Yellow-headed	*(Rryy)*

Females:

	3 Red-headed	*(ROYY; ROYy; ROYy)*
	4 Black-headed	*(rOYY; rOYy; rOYy; rOyy)*
	1 Yellow-headed	*(ROyy)*

TABLE 16

The outcomes of matings between a Red-headed male *(RrYy)* and a Black-headed female *(rOYy)*. Each parent can produce four types of sperm or egg and these are cast as a 4×4 matrix in order to work out all possible combinations (i.e. fusions between sperm and egg).

| | | *Female: eggs* | | | |
		rY	*ry*	*OY*	*Oy*
	RY	*RrYY*	*RrYy*	*ROYY*	*ROYy*
Male:	*Ry*	*RrYy*	*Rryy*	*ROYy*	*ROyy*
sperms	*rY*	*rrYY*	*rrYy*	*rOYY*	*rOYy*
	ry	*rrYy*	*rryy*	*rOYy*	*rOyy*

Overall, there are 54 possible matings each with a different expectation; their results are summarised below. The following abbreviations are used: RH = red-headed; BH = black-headed; YH = yellow-headed; ♂ = male, ♀ = female. Note that proportions of offspring are expressed in percentages.

Mating No.	Parents	Offspring (per cent)
1	RH ♂ *(RRYY)* × RH ♀ *(ROYY)*	♂ : 50 RH *(RRYY)* ♀ : 50 RH *(ROYY)*

Mating No.	Parents	Offspring (per cent)
2	RH ♂ *(RRYY)* × RH ♀ *(ROYy)*	♂: 25 RH *(RRYY)*; 25 RH *(RRYy)* ♀: 25 RH *(ROYY)*; 25 RH *(ROYy)*
3	RH ♂ *(RRYY)* × YH ♀ *(ROyy)*	♂: 50 RH *(RRYy)* ♀: 50 RH *(ROYy)*
4	RH ♂ *(RRYY)* × BH ♀ *(rOYY)*	♂: 50 RH *(RrYY)* ♀: 50 RH *(ROYY)*
5	RH ♂ *(RRYY)* × BH ♀ *(rOYy)*	♂: 25 RH *(RrYY)*; 25 RH *(RrYy)* ♀: 25 RH *(ROYY)*; 25 RH *(ROYy)*
6	RH ♂ *(RRYY)* × BH ♀ *(rOyy)*	♂: 50 RH *(RrYy)* ♀: 50 RH *(ROYy)*
7	RH ♂ *(RRYy)* × RH ♀ *(ROYY)*	♂: 25 RH *(RRYY)*: 25 RH *(RRYy)* ♀: 25 RH *(ROYY)*; 25 RH *(ROYy)*
8	RH ♂ *(RRYy)* × RH ♀ *(ROYy)*	♂: 12.5 RH *(RRYY)*; 25 RH *(RRYy)*; 12.5 YH *(RRyy)* ♀: 12.5 RH *(ROYY)*; 25 RH *(ROYy)*; 12.5 YH *(ROyy)*
9	RH ♂ *(RRYy)* × YH ♀ *(ROyy)*	♂: 25 RH *(RRYy)*; 25 YH *(RRyy)* ♀: 25 RH *(ROYy)*; 25 YH *(ROyy)*
10	RH ♂ *(RRYy)* × BH ♀ *(rOYY)*	♂: 25 RH *(RrYY)*; 25 RH *(RrYy)* ♀: 25 RH *(ROYY)*; 25 RH *(ROYy)*
11	RH ♂ *(RRYy)* × BH ♀ *(rOYy)*	♂: 12.5 RH *(RrYY)*; 12.5 RH *(RrYy)*; 12.5 YH *(Rryy)* ♀: 12.5 RH *(ROYY)*; 12.5 RH *(ROYy)*; 12.5 YH *(ROyy)*
12	RH ♂ *(RRYy)* × BH ♀ *(rOyy)*	♂: 25 RH *(RrYy)*; 25 YH *(Rryy)* ♀: 25 RH *(ROYy)*; 25 YH *(ROyy)*
13	YH ♂ *(RRyy)* × RH ♀ *(ROYY)*	♂: 50 RH *(RRYy)* ♀: 50 RH *(ROYy)*
14	YH ♂ *(RRyy)* × RH ♀ *(ROYy)*	♂: 25 RH *(RRYy)*; 25 YH *(RRyy)* ♀: 25 RH *(ROYy)*; 25 YH *(ROyy)*
15	YH ♂ *(RRyy)* × YH ♀ *(ROyy)*	♂: 50 YH *(RRyy)* ♀: 50 YH *(ROyy)*
16	YH ♂ *(RRyy)* × BH ♀ *(rOYY)*	♂: 50 RH *(RrYy)* ♀: 50 RH *(ROYy)*

Mating No.	Parents	Offspring (per cent)
17	YH ♂ *(RRyy)* × BH ♀ *(rOYy)*	♂: 25 RH *(RrYy);* 25 YH *(Rryy)* ♀: 25 RH *(ROYv);* 25 YH *(ROyy)*
18	YH ♂ *(RRyy)* × BH ♀ *(rOyy)*	♂: 50 YH *(Rryy)* ♀: 50 YH *(ROyy)*
19	RH ♂ *(RrYY)* × RH ♀ *(ROYY)*	♂: 25 RH *(RRYY);* 25 RH *(RrYY)* ♀: 25 RH *(ROYY);* 25 BH *(rOYY)*
20	RH ♂ *(RrYY)* × RH ♀ *(ROYy)*	♂: 12.5 RH *(RRYY);* 12.5 RH *(RRYy)* 12.5 RH *(RrYy);* 12.5 RH *(RrYY)* ♀: 12.5 RH *(ROYY);* 12.5 RH *(ROYy)* 12.5 BH *(rOYY);* 12.5 BH *(rOYy)*
21	RH ♂ *(RrYY)* × YH ♀ *(ROyy)*	♂: 25 RH *(RRYy);* 25 RH *(RrYy)* ♀: 25 RH *(ROYy);* 25 BH *(rOYy)*
22	RH ♂ *(RrYY)* × BH ♀ *(rOYY)*	♂: 25 RH *(RrYY);* 25 BH *(rrYY)* ♀: 25 RH *(ROYY);* 25 BH *(rOYY)*
23	RH ♂ *(RrYY)* × BH ♀ *(rOYy)*	♂: 12.5 RH *(RrYY);* 12.5 RH *(RrYy);* 12.5 BH *(rrYY);* 12.5 BH *(rrYy)* ♀: 12.5 RH *(ROYY);* 12.5 RH *(ROYy);* 12.5 BH *(rOYY);* 12.5 BH *(rOYy)*
24	RH ♂ *(RrYY)* × BH ♀ *(rOyy)*	♂: 25 RH *(RrYy);* 25 BH *(rrYy)* ♀: 25 RH *(ROYy);* 25 BH *(rOYy)*
25	RH ♂ *(RrYy)* × RH ♀ *(ROYY)*	♂: 12.5 RH *(RRYY);* 12.5 RH *(RrYY);* 12.5 RH *(RrYy);* 12.5 RH *(RRYy)* ♀: 12.5 RH *(ROYY);* 12.5 RH *(ROYy);* 12.5 BH *(rOYY);* 12.5 BH *(rOYy)*
26	RH ♂ *(RrYy)* × RH ♀ *(ROYy)*	♂: 6.25 RH *(RRYY);* 12.5 RH *(RrYy);* 12.5 RH *(RRYy);* 6.25 RH *(RrYY)* 6.25 YH *(RRyy);* 6.25 YH *(Rryy)* ♀: 6.25 RH *(ROYY);* 12.5 RH *(ROYy);* 6.25 YH *(ROyy);* 6.25 BH *(rOYY);* 12.5 BH *(rOYy);* 6.25 BH *(rOyy)*
27	RH ♂ *(RrYy)* × YH ♀ *(ROyy)*	♂: 12.5 RH *(RRYy);* 12.5 RH *(RrYy);* 12.5 YH *(RRyy);* 12.5 YH *(Rryy)* ♀: 12.5 RH *(ROYy);* 12.5 YH *(ROyy);*

Mating No.	Parents	Offspring (per cent)
28	RH ♂ *(RrYy)* × BH ♀ *(rOYY)*	12.5 BH *(rOYy)*; 12.5 BH *(rOyy)* ♂: 12.5 RH *(RrYY)*; 12.5 RH *(RrYy)*; 12.5 BH *(rrYY)*; 12.5 BH *(rrYy)* ♀: 12.5 RH *(ROYY)*; 12.5 RH *(ROYy)*; 12.5 BH *(rOYY)*; 12.5 BH *(rOYy)*
29	RH ♂ *(RrYy)* × BH ♀ *(rOYy)*	♂: 6.25 RH *(RrYY)*; 6.25 RH *(RrYy)*; 12.5 YH *(Rryy)*; 6.25 BH *(rrYY)*; 6.25 BH *(rryy)*; 12.5 BH *(rrYy)* ♀: 6.25 RH *(ROYY)*; 12.5 RH *(ROYy)*; 6.25 YH *(ROyy)*; 6.25 BH *(rOYY)*; 12.5 BH *(rOYy)*; 6.25 BH *(rOyy)*
30	RH ♂ *(RrYy)* × BH ♀ *(rOyy)*	♂: 12.5 RH *(RrYy)*; 12.5 YH *(Rryy)*; 12.5 BH *(rrYy)*; 12.5 BH *(rryy)* ♀: 12.5 RH *(ROYy)*; 12.5 YH *(ROyy)*; 12.5 BH *(rOYy)*; 12.5 BH *(rOyy)*
31	YH ♂ *(Rryy)* × RH ♀ *(ROYY)*	♂: 25 RH *(RRYy)*; 25 RH *(RrYy)*; ♀: 25 RH *(ROYy)*; 25 BH *(rOYy)*
32	YH ♂ *(Rryy)* × RH ♀ *(ROYy)*	♂: 12.5 RH *(RRYy)*; 12.5 RH *(RrYy)*; 12.5 YH *(RRyy)*; 12.5 YH *(Rryy)* ♀: 12.5 RH *(ROYy)*; 12.5 YH *(ROyy)*; 12.5 BH *(rOyy)*; 12.5 BH *(rOYy)*
33	YH ♂ *(Rryy)* × YH ♀ *(ROyy)*	♂: 25 YH *(RRyy)*; 25 YH *(Rryy)* ♀: 25 YH *(ROyy)*; 25 BH *(rOyy)*
34	YH ♂ *(Rryy)* × BH ♀ *(rOYY)*	♂: 25 RH *(RrYy)*; 25 BH *(rrYy)* ♀: 25 RH *(ROYy)*; 25 BH *(rOYy)*
35	YH ♂ *(Rryy)* × BH ♀ *(rOYy)*	♂: 12.5 RH *(RrYy)*; 12.5 YH *(Rryy)*; 12.5 BH *(rrYy)*; 12.5 BH *(rryy)* ♀: 12.5 RH *(ROYy)*; 12.5 YH *(ROyy)*; 12.5 BH *(rOyy)*; 12.5 BH *(rOYy)*
36	YH ♂ *(Rryy)* × BH ♀ *(rOyy)*	♂: 25 YH *(Rryy)*; 25 BH *(rryy)* ♀: 25 YH *(ROyy)*; 25 BH *(rOyy)*
37	BH ♂ *(rrYY)* × RH ♀ *(ROYY)*	♂: 50 RH *(RrYY)* ♀: 50 BH *(rOYY)*

Mating No.	Parents	Offspring (per cent)
38	BH ♂ *(rrYY)* ×	♂: 25 RH *(RrYY)*; 25 RH *(RrYy)*
	RH ♀ *(ROYy)*	♀: 25 BH *(rOYY)*; 25 BH *(rOYy)*
39	BH ♂ *(rrYY)* ×	♂: 50 RH *(RrYy)*
	YH ♀ *(ROyy)*	♀: 50 BH *(rOYy)*
40	BH ♂ *(rrYY)* ×	♂: 50 BH *(rrYY)*
	BH ♀ *(rOYY)*	♀: 50 BH *(rOYY)*
41	BH ♂ *(rrYY)* ×	♂: 25 BH *(rrYY)*; 25 BH *(rrYy)*
	BH ♀ *(rOYy)*	♀: 25 BH *(rOYY)*; 25 BH *(rOYy)*
42	BH ♂ *(rrYY)* ×	♂: 50 BH *(rrYy)*
	BH ♀ *(rOyy)*	♀: 50 BH *(rOYy)*
43	BH ♂ *(rrYy)* ×	♂: 25 RH *(RrYY)*; 25 RH *(RrYy)*
	RH ♀ *(ROYY)*	♀: 25 BH *(rOYy)*; 25 BH *(rOYY)*
44	BH ♂ *(rrYy)* ×	♂: 12.5 RH *(RrYY)*; 25 RH *(RrYy)*;
	RH ♀ *(ROYy)*	12.5 YH *(Rryy)*
		♀: 12.5 BH *(rOYY)*; 25 BH *(rOYy)*;
		12.5 BH *(rOyy)*
45	BH ♂ *(rrYy)* ×	♂: 25 RH *(RrYy)*; 25 YH *(Rryy)*
	YH ♀ *(ROyy)*	♀: 25 BH *(rOYy)*; 25 BH *(rOyy)*
46	BH ♂ *(rrYy)* ×	♂: 25 BH *(rrYY)*; 25 BH *(rrYy)*
	BH ♀ *(rOYY)*	♀: 25 BH *(rOYY)*; 25 BH *(rOYy)*
47	BH ♂ *(rrYy)* ×	♂: 12.5 BH *(rrYY)*; 25 BH *(rrYy)*;
	BH ♀ *(rOYy)*	12.5 BH *(rryy)*
		♀: 12.5 BH *(rOYY)*; 25 BH *(rOYy)*;
		12.5 BH *(rOyy)*
48	BH ♂ *(rrYy)* ×	♂: 25 BH *(rrYy)*; 25 BH *(rryy)*
	BH ♀ *(rOyy)*	♀: 25 BH *(rOYy)*; 25 BH *(rOyy)*
49	BH ♂ *(rryy)* ×	♂: 50 RH *(RrYy)*
	RH ♀ *(ROYY)*	♀: 50 BH *(rOYy)*
50	BH ♂ *(rryy)* ×	♂: 25 RH *(RrYy)*; 25 YH *(Rryy)*
	RH ♀ *(ROYy)*	♀: 25 BH *(rOYy)*; 25 BH *(rOyy)*
51	BH ♂ *(rryy)* ×	♂: 50 YH *(Rryy)*
	YH ♀ *(ROyy)*	♀: 50 BH *(rOyy)*

Mating No.	Parents	Offspring (per cent)
52	BH ♂ *(rryy)* ×	♂ : 50 BH *(rrYy)*
	BH ♀ *(rOYY)*	♀ : 50 BH *(rOYy)*
53	BH ♂ *(rryy)* ×	♂ : 25 BH *(rrYy)*; 25 BH *(rryy)*
	BH ♀ *(rOYy)*	♀ : 25 BH *(rOYy)*; 25 BH *(rOyy)*
54	BH ♂ *(rryy)* ×	♂ : 50 BH *(rryy)*
	BH ♀ *(rOyy)*	♀ : 50 BH *(rOyy)*

Notes

1) All matings involving two black-headed parents produce 100 per cent black-headed young.

2) Several of the matings (e.g. 27, 29, 30, 35) result in young of all three head colours. They are not recommended, however. There are additional genetic factors (not considered here), which affect head colour in the female, and can result in intermediate head colours. Red- and yellow-headed females can, for instance, produce some black pigment, resulting in melanistic head colour (i.e. either red/black or yellow/black). Similarly, some red-headed females show yellow flecking. The incidence of these intermediate head colours is increased by crossing different colour varieties. Good strains of red- and yellow-headed birds are likely to be developed by selective breeding and restricting matings to individuals of the same head colour (particularly matings 1 and 15).

3) The potential number of red-headed males produced from all 54 matings is higher than the number of red-headed females (see above). This difference is reflected in the proportions of these birds in wild populations and captive ones (see Tables 1 and 18). In both cases, red-headed males are more numerous than red-headed females.

12 SELECTIVE BREEDING

Most aviculturists aim to improve the quality of their stock by selective breeding. Each season, they select the the best birds from those available and breed only from them. Effectively, the aim is to keep those genetic factors which are responsible for the 'desirable' characters in the stock and to eliminate those which control 'undesirable' ones. In this case, however, selection is for characters which are controlled by many pairs of factors, and it is not feasible to work out mating expectations of the kinds described in the previous chapter. It is necessary to be content with gradual improvement in qualities, such as size, colour, shape and fecundity, over several generations.

Selective breeding is only likely to yield significant results when the breeder has a reasonably large stock of birds and is prepared to devote many years to producing a superior strain. He must be systematic in his approach and ruthless in the choice of breeding pairs. There is no room for sentimentality if this means keeping inferior birds in the breeding stock.

OBJECTIVES: THE STANDARD GOULDIAN FINCH

The first essential requirement is to define the objectives. What kind of bird are we attempting to produce? Or, in other words, which qualities are we hoping to improve in our stock? This is an area in which avicultural and bird societies have important roles to play. It is up to them to recommend standards to which breeders can concentrate their efforts. A recommended standard, which encompasses type and colouration of the Gouldian Finch, and which is based on that produced by the Australian Finch Society (UK) is presented on pp. 114–116. It should be remembered , however that this standard does not include several traits, such as fertility, fecundity, success in self-rearing young and hardiness in outdoor aviaries, all of which are desirable qualities and could be aimed for in programmes of selective breeding.

METHODS OF SELECTION

Almost inevitably, the breeder will decide to select for several different qualities. There are three recognised techniques for doing this in animal husbandry.

1) Tandem selection. This method involves selecting for one quality at a time. The breeder improves one character, such as size, over several generations

and then, having seen an improvement in it, selects for another character, say fertility. The procedure can obviously be repeated for one character after another but it is clearly long term!

2) Selecting for several characters with independent levels. The breeder decides on those characters for which he wishes to select and then sets a minimum standard for each of them. These standards might be based on body weight, size or shape, fertility levels, clutch sizes, or colouration for parts of the plumage. The breeding stock includes only those individuals which meet *all* the minimum levels.

3) Selection by pointing. This method is similar to the previous one, except that a scheme of points is worked out for each of the qualities under consideration. One possible scheme, which is based partly on the standard Gouldian Finch but also includes some other qualities, is shown on pp. 116–117. Each bird is scored (pointed) for each of the qualities and its total score worked out. Those individuals which score the highest numbers of points qualify as next year's breeding stock. The pointing method has the virtue that it does not exclude birds which excel in several characters but fail to reach the minimum standard on one of them. It is usually considered to be the most efficient way of selecting stock. Tandem selection is usually considered to be the least efficient (Dr J.R. Bowman. *Introduction to Animal Breeding*, 1974, published by Edward Arnold).

INBREEDING, OUTBREEDING AND LINE-BREEDING

Selective breeding is likely to lead to some inbreeding, or at least the temptation to inbreed; that is to say, to mate closely-related individuals together, such as father to daughter, brother to sister, and cousin to cousin. In general, this is undesirable. Long experience with farm animals has shown that too much inbreeding can result in abnormalities appearing in the stock, and a general reduction in condition and quality. Indeed, some closely inbred strains have died out altogether because eventually they failed to propagate at all. The reason is probably that many 'undesirable' qualities are controlled by genetically recessive factors and can therefore be carried in a single dose (i.e. as splits), without being expressed in the carrier. A parent is, however, likely to pass on such factors to several of its offspring and, if the brother mates with sister or father with daughter, there is a good chance that the undesirable recessives will come together in a double dose in some of the young. The character will therefore be expressed in them.

113

The generally recognised solution to this problem is to line-breed. This is in essence a mild form of inbreeding. A strain is developed from a group of birds by confining matings to distant relatives. Eventually all of the birds will become related to one another to at least some extent but matings between closely-related ones are always avoided. The breeder can select strongly for desirable qualities in the strain, and if it begins to show the deleterious effects of inbreeding or if it lacks in some quality, such as size or fertility, outbreeding is possible.

This involves mating totally unrelated birds, which excel in the needed qualities, with members of the strain. An added advantage of occasional outbreeding (but one which is probably over-estimated) is that it sometimes results in a phenomenon known as *heterosis* or *hybrid vigour*. Crosses between members of two different strains may produce young which are superior in quality to both of them. A possible explanation is that the dominant genes of both parents appear in the offspring, and they swamp any undesirable recessive characters which have built up in either of the parental strains. In general, however, outbreeding should be used with extreme caution. It can just as easily reintroduce undesirable traits which have been carefully eliminated from the strain over the years of painstaking selection, as desirable ones. Avoid in particular the temptation of outbreeding with a bird which is good in appearance but is of unknown pedigree. It may be carrying all sorts of undesirable characters as recessives in its make-up and these, once they have been introduced into the strain, could take years to eliminate.

THE STANDARD GOULDIAN FINCH

This is based on the breeding standard recommended by the Australian Finch Society (UK).

Black-headed Male

Type. The body should be substantial but not 'cobby' and it should taper elegantly to the tail. The outline, taking a line from the beak over the crown, nape, back, rump and tail should be smooth and flowing. Breaks in it caused by, for example, nipped necks, dropped or cocked tails, are faults. The line from the lower mandible over the chin, throat, chest, abdomen and vent and tail should also be smooth.

The length is approximately 14 cm ($5\frac{1}{2}$ in). Small birds often lack vigour and do not show well, but excessive size is also a fault.

The wings should be held close to the body and the tips should meet at the upper tail coverts. Dropped and crossed wings are faults.

The two central feathers of the tail should be elongated, separated and should run parallel to one another. Tail feathers which run together or are splayed are faults. The tail wires should be as long as possible but the lengths of the other tail feathers should be in proportion to the length of the body.

Colouration. Colour is of equal if not more importance than type. The forehead, crown, ear coverts, chin and throat should be deep black with a slightly glossy sheen. A line of turquoise blue extends from the throat right round the back of the head, encircling the area of black. The edge between the turquoise band and the black should be sharply defined. The band should also be sharply defined from the breast colour but should extend into and merge with the green of the side of the neck and the mantle.

The mantle and back should be green but with a gold suffusion. This is more intensive on the mantle and in the area approaching the rump.

The wing coverts should be dark green with a slightly glossy sheen. The primaries should be dark grey, almost black, with a lighter edging to the flight feathers.

The deep purple breast patch should extend from the turquoise band to a line (the bloodline) running across the chest; this should be clearcut and have a reddish tinge. The area below it should be deep buttercup yellow, gradually fading to white in the area of the vent. The under tail coverts should be white. The rump and upper tail coverts should be light sky blue. Some frosting on the edges of the feathers of the upper tail coverts is acceptable. The tail should be black.

The upper and lower mandibles of the beak should be pearly white with either a red or a yellow tip. The legs are flesh-coloured; the nails horn-coloured. The eyes should be black with a thin flesh-coloured ring.

Black-headed Female

The standard is the same as that for the male, except that females tend to be 'heavier' in build so that a 'cobbier' bird than the male is desirable. The two central tail feathers should not be as long as those in the male. The plumage of the female is duller and lacks the gloss of that of the male. The purple breast patch in particular is paler than the male's, and the mantle and back lack the gold suffusion.

Red-headed Male and Female

As for the black-headed birds, except that the forehead, crown and ear coverts are deep scarlet red. The colouration should be even with no black or orange flecking.

Yellow-headed Male and Female

There is some evidence that there are two genetically true breeding types of yellow-head, and they should therefore be given different standards. The standards of both are the same as that for red-headed birds except that the red is replaced by either old gold orange or deep golden buttercup yellow.

White-breasted Male and Female

As for normal birds but the purple breast patch is replaced by one of clear intense white. These birds tend to a lighter colouration which is a fault.

POINTING SYSTEM FOR STOCK SELECTION

The scheme chosen will depend on the qualities for which selection is being made. The one described below is for general improvement of stock. Each bird is awarded up to a maximum of 100 points as follows.

Size: 20 points. At this stage in the development of the Gouldian Finch as a domestic species, large size is probably of more importance than it will be in the future. At present large birds are generally more vigorous and productive than smaller ones, which are often the products of unselective matings and 'factory breeding'. It is nevertheless important that future generations of aviculturists do not produce ugly 'giants'.

Shape: 25 points. Points are allocated to different parts of the body according to the difficulty in achieving the objectives set out in the standard Gouldian Finch:

Body	13 points
Tail	9
Wings	3

Colouration: 30 points. More points are given to this category than to any of the others because colour is the outstanding attribute of this species:

Head	10 points
Breast	8

Rump	7
Back	3
Rest of Body	2

Family History: 25 points. This is an assessment of the parentage of the birds (and requires good record keeping):

Overall quality of parental line	10 points
Fertility	5
Disease resistance	5
Ability to self-rear	5

New mutations arise from time to time in cage birds and, when they result in attractive colour varieties, they are highly sought after. This has led, for example, to the establishment of many different varieties of canaries, budgerigars and lovebirds. Mutations which affect colouration nearly always arise from deficiencies in the mechanisms for producing colours (see Chapter 1). The white-breasted mutation in the Gouldian Finch (Plate 7), for instance, is one in which birds cannot produce pigments in the breast feathers. Mutations can also result in an increase in the intensity of pigments but almost never in the 'invention' of new colours. Several domestic varieties of canary have red pigments in the plumage, which never occur in wild canaries, but this innovation is due not to a mutation but to hybridisation. It is the result of crossing the canary with the Red Siskin, which does manufacture red pigment in its feathers. The hybrids have inherited the ability from the Siskin, and further crosses with canaries have incorporated it into various strains.

THEORETICAL AND ACTUAL MUTATIONS OF THE GOULDIAN FINCH

It is possible. given a knowledge of the mechanisms responsible for feather colouration in the Gouldian Finch, to predict the mutations which will occur. This can be done by considering the effects of failure of each of the mechanisms in turn. This will lead to the subtraction of a particular colour from all or part of the body, such as the breast or the back and wings. These colour-producing mechanisms are discussed more fully in Chapter 1, but, at this point, it is worth recalling that the remarkable feather colours in the Gouldian Finch are due entirely to structural blue and four colour pigments: eumelanin (black), phaeomelanin (reddish-brown), astaxantin (red) and lutein (yellow). The last mentioned of these, lutein, is not actually manufactured in the body but taken up from the food. It turns out that many of the possible mutations have already occurred, although so far only one of them, the white-breasted, is well-established. The following do nevertheless exist.

Lutino

These birds lack the ability to manufacture either of the melanins (eumelanin or phaeomelanin). Their only colours are therefore red (due to astaxantin), yellow (lutein) and white (no pigments). The red-headed lutino has the usual red-head but yellow wings and body; the breast patch is white. They have often been described as albinos but this name should be reserved for the mutation, which may not have occurred yet, in which no pigments are formed; the plumage will then be uniformly white.

Dilute-backed (Plate 8)

This variety does not manufacture melanin in the feathers of the back and wings and, since these cannot therefore produce structural blue, they are yellow, or light greenish-yellow, in colour. The mutation also affects the head plumage of the normally black-headed form; it is grey (see Plate 8). Other parts of the body are as intense in colour as the normal Gouldian Finch.

Blue-backed (Plate 9)

This mutant cannot take up lutein from its food and therefore lacks any yellow pigment. It is also devoid of the red astaxantin since this is manufactured from lutein (see above). The back and wings, whose green in the normal bird is the result of the combined effects of yellow lutein and structural blue, become blue. The belly is white instead of yellow and the head colour, in the red- and yellow-headed varieties, is brown.

Pastel

There is a general dilution of colours.

Breast colouration

Lilac-, cobalt- and blue-breasted varieties (Plate 10) have occurred in addition to the white-breasted mutation.

SUCCESSES AND FAILURES WITH MUTATIONS

Most attempts to establish new mutations have resulted in disappointment and failure. There is, however, one notable success story: that of the white-breasted variety. This mutation, like many of the others, has occurred independently in different countries. It was recorded in Australian aviaries in the mid-1950s but, although aviculturists bred it there for several years, the strain eventually died out. There were reports at about the same time of white-breasts in South Africa, and the South African National Cage Bird Association even went as far as including it in its schedule for 1962. The mutation was, however, of dubious status until Mr F. Barnicoat obtained two white-breasted males from a pet shop in Johannesburg in January 1965. The manager, realising that he had something special, had the foresight to offer them to Mr Barnicoat so that he could attempt to establish the strain.

manager, realising that he had something special, had the foresight to offer them to Mr Barnicoat so that he could attempt to establish the strain.

Mr Barnicoat, who describes his experiences with the mutant in an article in *Australian Aviculture* (April 1967, pp. 49–50), paired the white-breasted males with normal females from his own strain. One pair went down to nest and eventually produced a brood of five which fledged in April 1965. A second brood of three left the nest in July. The offsprings moulted into six red-headed males and two black-headed females, all with normal purple breasts. He feared that this might mean that the mutation was not a genuine one but it turned out that it was a recessive one and that the young were therefore split for it. He crossed the original white-breasted males with two black-headed females from the previous round (daughters of one of them) in 1966, and, in all, 10 young were reared. The first white-breasted youngster moulted in September and subsequently six of the others revealed white breasts when they moulted out of juvenile plumage. There were four white-breasted females (three black-headed and one red-headed) and three males (one black-headed and two red-headed). The three remaining young had purple breasts (but would have been splits; see Chapter 11).

The white-breasted variety was soon imported, and is now widely available in Europe and the USA. It was, for example, first imported into the United Kingdom from South Africa by Mr R. A. Eggington (described in an article in *Foreign Birds* 1969, which is reprinted in *The Grassfinch*, 1984, Vol. 8, p. 40). He obtained two white-breasted males and two splits (one male and one female) in February 1969. At least one white-breasted bird was reared from them in that year. In March 1970, Mr Eric Cooper and two other aviculturists imported five pairs of white-breasted birds and splits, also from South Africa. They bred successfully from them and, within only a few years, the mutation was widely available. The first records of white-breasted birds in a survey of

21 breeders in the United Kingdom were in 1976 (Fig. 21). They have been available ever since.

The dilute-backed mutation seems close to becoming established in Australia. Mr Ray Murray *(Australian Aviculture,* January 1973, pp. 4–7) describes how it originally turned up in the aviaries of two Queenslanders in about 1945. Murray was able to obtain a small number of them, and seemed to have the mutation well on the way to being established when, in 1970, an unknown disease destroyed about 90 per cent of his stock. There were further problems in 1973 and he eventually finished up with only one split male. Despite this, stocks have been built up again and aviculturists in both Melbourne and Brisbane are breeding them.

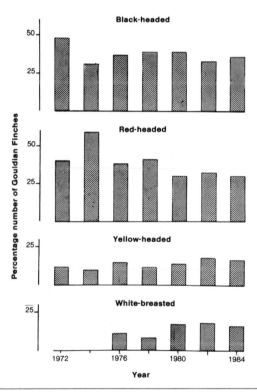

Fig. 21 *Changes in the proportions of Gouldian Finches of the three head colours and of white-breasted birds in the stock of 21 breeders in the United Kingdom from 1972 until 1984.*

Attempts to establish a strain of lutinos have so far been unsuccessful in Australia. The mutation has appeared separately in South Australia and Queensland but none of the breeders have been able to establish it. The most distressing story is that of Mr A. H. Catt of New South Wales. He started with a lutino which had been wild-trapped and was able to create what seemed to be a viable stock from it. Unfortunately, a thief broke into his aviaries and took all of the mutants. Lutinos evidently suffer from poor eyesight, as a result of a lack of normal eye pigments, and there is a heavy mortality of newly-fledged birds. According to some accounts, the young also lack the normal luminescent mouth markings and their parents are reluctant to feed them.

The blue-backed mutation has also appeared independently in different countries. Mr Ray Johnson (*Australian Aviculture*, January 1953, p. 8) reports that it occurred in the stock of a number of Sydney breeders, although there were arguments about its status. Some aviculturists believed that it was not a mutation at all but resulted from lutein deficiences in diet. Be this as it may, blue-backed birds do not appear to have been established in Australia. The mutation has nevertheless occurred in Europe, and in this case it is undoubtedly genuine. It is, for example, being bred by some Dutch aviculturists. They too are making good progress with the pastel mutation.

Blue-breasted Gouldian Finches are becoming increasingly available in the USA, and seem well established in the aviaries of Dr Herschel Frey. Some have also been imported into the UK, where the lilac-breasted variety is also kept by several breeders.

LOST MUTATIONS

Mr A. J. Mobbs (*The Grassfinch*, 1980, Vol. 4, No. 6, pp. 6–8) describes three unusual mutations which have been reported in the United Kingdom but have evidently been lost to aviculture. One of the most curious, and difficult to understand in terms of the pigments involved, is a green-headed variety. Mr Leonard Webber (*Avicultural Magazine*, 1949, p. 190) bred six of these birds, which varied in head colour from green, to green on black, to a copper metallic hue with green. The Keston Foreign Bird Farm (*Avicultural Magazine*, 1938, p. 18) bred a hen with a blue streak down the centre of its breast. Those parts of the plumage which are normally yellow were greenish-yellow. Finally, Mrs Kathleen Wilson-Jones (*Avicultural Magazine*, 1936, p. 202) describes a red-headed male which was melanistic and also pied. It was predominantly black, but had a red head, orange belly and purple breast (which was heavily marked with black feathers), together with a few dark green olive feathers on otherwise black wings.

Other 'lost' mutations have occurred in Australia; they have been described in an article by Mr Ray Murray *(Australian Aviculture,* January 1973, pp. 4–7). Fawn young appeared in the aviaries of both Mr Keith Thompson of Glenhuntly and Mr Lou Koenig of Ararat, but neither breeder was able to rear them to adulthood. Similarly, Mr Phil Frampton was unable to establish a strain from a pied red-headed male. 'Avian' writes of an interesting mutation in *Australian Aviculture* (September 1966, pp. 121–122) as follows:

But now I do have something different . . . a bird which is so different that it has to be seen to be believed, and while it is not of my breeding, I should like to describe it.

A mutant Gouldian hen, it bears little resemblance to the normal Gouldian except for body shape. Both wings and back are pale cream, the breast which is normally purple has become pure white as is the tail and the rest of the body is pale cream except the head which is light tangerine colour sparsely flecked with grey. The eyes are not pink as in the albino but dark brown and the legs are normal pink.

The person from whom I purchased this bird (and who wishes to remain just as anonymous as I do at this stage) has had these mutants for four years. As far as he can remember, they were the progeny of a pair of normal black headed Gouldians but as the flight in which they are housed is about 50 feet by 20 feet heavily planted and is shared with some dozens of red, yellow, and black headed Gouldians, the strain has been lost to a great degree through their breeding with the various normals. The cocks of this mutation as far as I can see do carry some colour as there are some birds in this huge flight obviously cocks whose wings, backs and bodies are cream but have a bright red or tangerine head while the breast is a subdued but attractive violet. I imagine there are about eight or ten pure mutants altogether as well as about twenty splits showing various degrees of digression from normal colour. Some are almost pure mutant except for green wings, whilst others give the impression of normals which have been quickly dipped in some bleaching agent and have lost perhaps 40% of their colour all over.

ESTABLISHING A NEW MUTATION

As the foregoing accounts emphasise, establishing a new variety is a job for the expert. The temptation for the inexperienced aviculturist to experiment with rearing methods and, at the same time, to attempt to establish a new mutation is understandable but it is an unrealistic objective. One reason for the high failure rate is that many mutants have defects other than those concerned with plumage colour and may be struggling simply to keep alive. Only the experienced aviculturist is likely to be successful in persuading such birds to breed.

Someone must nevertheless take the responsibility and the following guidelines, which are similar in many respects to the procedures adopted by Mr Barnicoat (see above), are recommended.

1) Consider rearing young under Bengalese Finch foster-parents, making sure that a reliable strain of these birds is available. Although we have advised caution in the use of foster-rearing in Chapters 5 and 9, it is justified here since it enables many more clutches than would normally be possible to be reared from a single pair of birds.

2) Matings must be under controlled conditions (cage breeding). Recessive mutations will be temporarily 'lost' in splits in colonies and there is likely to be no way of telling which birds are split for the mutation and which are not.

3) The mutation may have been carried as a recessive for generations without showing itself, and may not have arisen in the first birds actually to exhibit it. It follows that close relatives of the mutant, including its parents, may be split for it. Valuable matings which are not normally advised, since they lead to inbreeding (see Chapter 12), are therefore those between close relatives. There is a chance that they will yield more mutants.

4) Mutants should be crossed with good quality normals to improve the stock. If, as is usually the case, the mutation is recessive, the offspring will be split for it. The next round of matings should be between splits and mutants. Mating split to split, and split to normal, should be attempted only as a last resort because a proportion of the young from them (25 and 50 per cent respectively) will be normals, and they will be indistinguishable from the splits.

5) In view of the potentially large numbers of Gouldian Finch mutations, indiscriminate matings between them should be avoided. It is desirable for avicultural societies to recommend standards for accepted varieties and discourage attempts to interbreed them.

14   DISEASES AND RELATED PROBLEMS

Small finches are difficult to treat once they have contracted disease. Their metabolic rates are so high that disease may reach its climax in a matter of hours rather than days. The bird which was looking 'off colour' on one day may be beyond saving by the next. It is also unfortunate that the treatment of bird diseases is a highly specialised aspect of animal husbandry and one in which there are few experts. There are even few veterinary surgeons who consider themselves to be well versed in this branch of their subject.

Fig. 22 *A sick Gouldian Finch.*

There are nevertheless two important safeguards which can be taken by the aviculturist to reduce the chances of a major outbreak of disease. The first, and most obvious, is to keep the birdroom, cages and utensils scrupulously clean. It is advisable to follow the guidelines for hygiene which are set out in Chapter 5, and to make sure that food and water are always clean. Second, the birds should be inspected regularly for early signs of illness. The hunched 'fluffed' posture (Fig. 22), often with the head beneath the wing, and general listlessness, are sure signs that something is wrong. Watch too for the symptom known as 'going light', in which the bird becomes thinner and thinner and almost literally wastes away.

If illness is detected early enough, there is a good chance of curing it. An integral part of treatment is usually to supply additional heat which gives the bird's own defence mechanisms against disease a chance to take over, to the point where it may recover without much further help. Rather than catch up unhealthy birds and cause them additional stress, some aviculturists simply raise the temperature of the birdroom by a few degrees, to say 30°C (85°F), when they first suspect that something is wrong. When individual treatment is necessary, this can be given in a hospital cage, which is heated by a 40 or 60 watt bulb. Ideally, this cage should be kept somewhere other than in the birdroom so that the diseased bird is quarantined from the rest of the stock, and there is less risk of cross-infection from it.

Some relatively common ailments can be diagnosed and treated by the aviculturist, but veterinary advice should be sought if the cause of a disease is not obvious or if it seems in danger of reaching epidemic proportions. The vet will be able to supply antibiotics and send corpses for pathological examination and tests. The most frequently encountered ailments of adult Gouldian Finches (problems with nestlings have been dealt with in Chapter 8), are considered below. We include recommended treatments, with dosages, where these have proved effective in the past but stress, in doing so, that avian medicine is a neglected subject and still in its early stages of development.

DIARRHOEA

This can be caused by a variety of diseases from a simple chill to avian cholera or typhoid. Many of them result from outbreaks of bacteria in the intestine, including those belonging to the groups *Escherichia*, *Pasteurella* and *Salmonella*, but one of these diseases, coccidiosis, is caused by an infection of protozoans (microscopic unicellular organisms). The most obvious symptom, in addition to the general lack of condition, is for the vent to become wet and soiled. The droppings themselves will be watery but may be white, yellowish, fawn or green, depending on the type of infection. Most of these diseases are highly contagious so that strict cleanliness and hygiene are necessary in the birdroom. Identification of the disease is a job for the expert but it is wise to treat birds with antibiotics from the outset.

A 'universal antibiotic cocktail mix' which has proved effective in the past consists of 0.4g *aureomycin* or *spectinomycin* or *terramycin*, together with 1.5ml of a 33 per cent solution of *sulphamezathine* in 56ml (2 fluid ounces) of water. This is provided in place of the birds' normal drinking water. The treatment is continued for five days.

Although the stock may appear to be clinically cured, there is always a danger of a second outbreak and it is wise therefore to keep a close watch on the birds for some time afterwards. Any reappearance of the symptoms should be treated in a similar fashion immediately.

CANKER

Canker is caused by a protozoan, *Trichomonas*. Although it is not a common infection among Gouldian Finches kept in temperate parts of the world, it is prevalent in countries where warm climates encourage aviculturists to keep their birds in outside aviaries. The symptoms in nestlings are described in Chapter 8. Infections in adult birds are more difficult to detect but are usually preceded by the usual signs of listlessness, perching in a fluffed posture, and going light. In severe cases, the birds have difficulty in breathing. Inspection of the insides of their mouths reveals white, sticky patches of exudate.

The universal cocktail mix of antibiotics, with dimetridazole (emtryl) added, has been used successfully for treatment. The source of most infections is from wild birds, which perch on the roofs of aviaries; covered aviaries reduce this potential hazard.

AIRSAC MITES

The airsac mite, *Sternostoma tracheacolum*, is a small arthropod which infects the lungs and airsacs of the bird. At one time this was the scourge of the breeder of Gouldian Finches, and the cause of many bird deaths and breeding problems. Eventually aviculturists realised that it responded to treatment with insecticides and developed various methods of combatting it. These included shaking the sick bird in a paper bag together with malathion dust!

In the earliest stages, birds which are infected with airsac mite will be breathless after activity and will cough. They frequently wipe their beaks across the perch. At more advanced stages, the infected birds will be listless, sit fluffed up, and will audibly wheeze and cough. Confirmation of the infection can be made by holding the finch close to the ear. A clicking noise will be heard as it breathes, together with a 'wet-sounding' wheeze.

Airsac mite can be eliminated from birdrooms by hanging pest strips of the kind used for killing houseflies. If a newly-purchased bird develops the symptoms, one of the pest strips could be hung at the back of its cage and left until there is no longer any evidence of infection. Care must be taken to use a small strip in this situation. The insecticide in it is also poisonous to birds and an overdose will kill the bird as well as its mites!

The treatment of aviary birds is based on the use of the insecticide carbaryl, which is mixed with seed. Mr M. D. Murray *(Australian Veterinary Journal,* 1966, Vol. 42, pp. 262–264) recommends that the dosage is 0.04g of carbaryl to 50g of seed. A small amount of cod liver oil or olive oil (1ml to 50g of seed) is

TABLE 17
The effects of treating airsac mite with carbaryl. The numbers of mites are shown in various parts of the body in five untreated control finches and five treated birds. (Data from M. D. Murray, *Australian Veterinary Journal,* 1966, Vol. 42, pp. 262–264.)

	Bird number	Trachea	Lungs	Airsac and abdomen	Total
			Number of mites		
Untreated controls	1	12	26	40	78
	2	38	62	40	140
	3	71	65	40	176
	4	24	20	30	74
	5	49	23	40	112
Treated finches	1	0	2	7	9
	2	0	0	1	1
	3	0	0	0	0
	4	0	1	0	1
	5	0	0	3	3

mixed with the seed before adding the carbaryl powder to ensure that it adheres to it, and is distributed evenly among it. The treated seed is presented to the birds for about 40 hours and then for periods of about a day, twice more, at weekly intervals. This is the maximum dose and should not be exceeded.

Mr Murray carried out an interesting experiment in which 10 immature Gouldian Finches, which had been bred from parents infected with airsac mite, were divided into two groups. One group was treated with carbaryl; the other group was untreated. After the treatment all of the birds were culled, dissected and various parts of the respiratory system examined for mites. It can be seen from the results presented in Table 17 that the treated group was almost completely clear of the parasite but that the untreated group was still heavily infected.

INTESTINAL WORMS

The damp floors of open aviaries are often breeding grounds for the thread worms *Ascaridia* and *Capillaria.* They infect the birds' intestines and cause general lack of condition. Again, they are not usually a problem in well-kept birdrooms, but can become so in outside aviaries, particularly in warm climates. Microscopic examination of a bird's droppings will reveal the worms' eggs. A small amount of the black portion of a fresh dropping is mixed with two or three drops of water and examined under the microscope at low magnification of about 80 or 100 times. The eggs of *Ascaridia* appear as steel-blue/grey ovals, each with two vacuoles resembling air bubbles in appearance. *Capillaria* eggs are smaller, yellow and have a bulge at each end, which is more easily seen under higher magnification.

Commercial preparations are available for avian treatment in Europe and the USA. The recommended way of dosing the Gouldian Finch is to give it usually one drop from an eye dropper. This is administered either by allowing the bird to bite the bottom of the dropper and then squeezing the bulb, or by holding the bird on its side and placing the drop in the corner of its beak so that it runs into it. Some aviculturists have successfully used *Panacur 2.5* which is widely available from agricultural merchants, and is normally used for the treatment of worms in cattle.It is added to the drinking water at the rate of one droplet of *Panacur 2.5* per 10ml of water. The dose should be repeated at six-weekly intervals until the problem is cleared.

Once stock has become heavily infected, eradication is difficult, particularly in planted aviaries where the damp soil provides an ideal refuge for the worms. The concrete floors of covered aviaries can be treated with a blow lamp. Utensils should be thoroughly washed and rinsed daily.

BALDNESS

This is a relatively common and unsightly problem in the Gouldian Finch. The affected bird normally loses feathers from the neck and head region and, in bad cases, becomes completely bald, bearing an unfortunate resemblance to a vulture. There may well be more than one cause for it and there is certainly no full agreement among aviculturists as to its treatment. Some believe that it is due to feather mites and claim to cure it with sprays or powders which contain insecticides. Others have had no success with this kind of treatment. Diet deficiency is another possible cause.

CLAW AND BEAK TRIMMING

The claws of birds kept in cages, and some in aviaries as well, become overgrown and require trimming periodically. This can be done with household nail clippers. The finch is held with its back against the palm of the hand and the little finger across its throat. The thumb and index finger are now used to hold and steady one of the legs. Each claw should be clipped below the red line where blood vessels end (i.e. cutting away only 'dead' tissue).

Occasionally a bird may suffer from one of the mandibles of the beak becoming elongated. This too requires trimming and, again, can be done with nail clippers. The bird is held firmly in the hand but this time with its head between the finger and thumb and the offending mandible trimmed back to its correct level.

15 DEVELOPMENT OF THE GOULDIAN FINCH IN CAPTIVITY

Since the Australian Government's ban on the export of its wildlife over twenty years ago, Gouldian Finches have been bred in large numbers in many parts of the world, including Europe, South Africa and the USA. These populations, which are kept outside Australia, have been maintained in total isolation of wild birds, and the species is therefore thoroughly domesticated. The situation is an interesting one because it presents a unique opportunity to investigate the early stages in a domestication process. Although man has been domesticating animals for hundreds of years, the process has never been documented and is poorly understood. Indeed, much of what has happened has been lost in the mists of time and we are unsure of the wild progenitors of several domestic species, including the horse and the dog.

DOMESTICATION

Most, if not all, domestic animals have undergone considerable change during their captive existences (see Fig. 23). There are basically two reasons for this. First, man deliberately selects for 'useful' qualities in many of his domestic animals. He has, for example, bred for egg-production in strains of domestic fowl and, as a result, has developed birds which, by natural standards, are little more than egg-laying machines. Similarly, he has produced some breeds of cattle which have abnormally high milk yields, and other breeds whose carcases are valuable for their meat. Varieties of dogs have been selectively bred for their fighting, hunting and guarding abilities . . . and so on. Pets and ornamental animals are subject to similar pressures but, in their cases, characters, such as size, shape and colouration, are often the ones on which selection is based. The second cause of change in domestic animals results from the conditions in which they are kept. These are usually quite different from the wild and may include, for example, changes in climatic conditions, provision of unnatural diets, enclosure within restricted spaces and over-crowding. Not surprisingly, most domestic animals are much more tolerant than their wild relatives of living in close proximity of another, and they also become tame to the approach of humans. They must, in addition, breed in very different circumstances from those in nature, and many domestic animals have heightened sexual responses. Several have, for instance, lost their seasonality of breeding and will reproduce at any time of the year.

The extent to which the Gouldian Finch has changed during its short history of domestication is being explored by a research team at the University

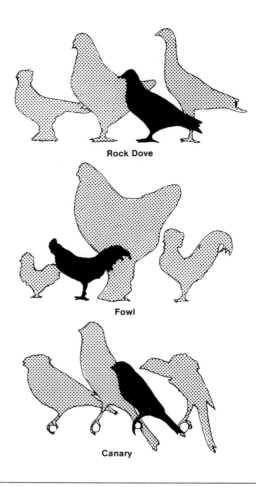

Fig. 23 *Changes in the shapes and relative sizes of three birds as a result of domestication; the Rock Dove, the Fowl and the Canary. The original wild-type forms are shown in black. (Based on a diagram by R. Sossinka in an article which appears in* Avian Biology, *1982, Vol. VI, pp 373–403. It is published by Academic Press and edited by D.S. Farner, J.R. King and K.C. Parkes.)*

of Newcastle-upon-Tyne (UK). Their first step has been to make comparisons of wild-caught and domestically-bred birds. The wild birds, which were exported from Western Australia under special licence, were compared with domestic individuals, which were bred at the University.

CHANGES IN THE GOULDIAN FINCH

The proportions of different head-colour varieties of the Gouldian Finch are quite different in domestic stock and wild birds. About 75 per cent of wild birds are black-headed and almost all of the remainder are red-headed; yellow-headed birds are rare (Table 18; see also Chapter 1). In captivity, however, the numbers of black-headed and red-headed birds are about equal, and yellow-headed birds make up about 19 per cent of the population. The most likely explanation for changes is that aviculturists have preferred to breed red-headed, and certainly yellow-headed, individuals because they are less common than black-headed ones – or perhaps because they are considered to be more attractive. The rarity factor is certainly an important one in ensuring

TABLE 18

The proportions of different head colours in wild and domestic birds. The information on wild birds is a summary of that in Table 1; that on domestic birds is based on a survey of 21 breeders.

	Black-headed		Red-headed		Yellow-headed	
	males	*females*	*males*	*females*	*males*	*females*
			Wild Birds			
Numbers	139	120	70	30	2	1
Totals	259		100		3	
Percentages	71.5		27.6		0.8	
			Domestic Birds			
Numbers	80	111	113	71	45	46
Totals	191		184		91	
Percentages	41.0		39.5		19.5	

the spread of a new mutation, once it has become established. The speed at which this happens can be extraordinary. The first white-breasted Gouldian Finches were, for example, imported into the United Kingdom in 1969 and 1970 (see Chapter 13) but, although they did not appear in most breeders' stocks until the mid-1970s, they accounted for nearly 15 per cent of birds kept by the early 1980s (see Fig. 21).

There is some evidence that the Gouldian Finch is increasing in size as a result of domestication. Domestic females measured by the Newcastle team were, in fact, only slightly heavier than those from the wild (2.5 per cent), but males were noticeably larger (17.5 per cent). The mean (average) weights were as follows.

Domestic females:	16.3g
Wild-caught females:	15.9g
Domestic males:	16.8g
Wild-caught males:	14.3g

It is not yet clear whether these differences have occurred because of deliberate selection for size by aviculturists (which certainly happens) or because factors, such as enriched diets and insufficient exercise, result in large individuals in captivity.

There were also differences in colour in the domestic and wild-caught birds, although these are difficult to interpret because of the natural variations in the colour of wild birds (see Chapter 1). It does nevertheless seem likely that aviculturists select for brightness of plumage. One of the differences observed in the Newcastle research was in the yellow of the feathers in the belly region, and this appears to illustrate the trend. The wild-trapped birds had relatively pale yellow bellies, whereas this part of the plumage in domestically-bred individuals was a brighter, rich golden-yellow. Similarly, the turquoise head bands of wild males were narrower and less conspicuous than those of their captive counterparts.

Comparisons of the songs of wild-caught and domestically-bred Gouldian Finches revealed no detectable differences, which was a surprising find in view of Dr Baptista's demonstration that Gouldian Finches sometimes learn the songs of the 'wrong' birds in captivity (see Chapter 10). One might have expected that the habit of foster-rearing Gouldian Finches under Bengalese Finches would have resulted in some abnormal song-learning, but evidently this was not so. It is interesting, however, that the Newcastle University team was able to record only one of the two contact calls, which are given by wild birds, in their domestic stock. Both groups regularly gave the 'ssit-ssit' call but only the wild ones gave the 'ssreeh' call (see Fig. 13). It seems that domestic birds have either lost this call from their vocal repertoire or no longer use it.

Wild birds were more active than domestic ones and showed pronounced peaks of activity in the early morning, at midday and in the late afternoon, before roosting (Fig. 24). The middle of the afternoon was a period of

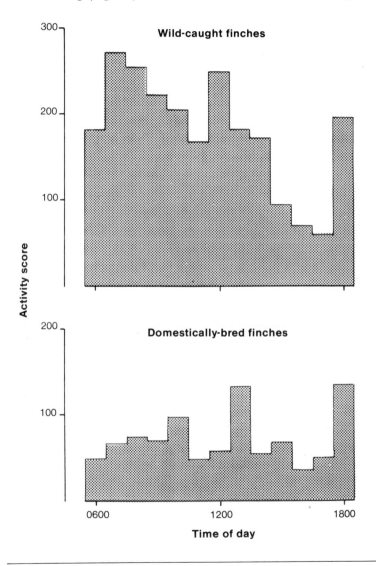

Fig. 24 *Activity (flying from perch to perch) in wild-caught Gouldian Finches and domestic ones throughout a full day, from 0600 until 1800.*

inactivity when the birds spent much of their time sleeping. Domestic birds were much less active than the wild ones in the early mornings, although they did have peaks of activity at midday and before roosting.

The most significant difference between the wild-caught and domestic birds was in their breeding performance. Pairs of birds were isolated in separate cages and allowed to lay clutches of eggs which were then transferred to Bengalese Finch foster-parents for rearing. This was done in order to ensure that all chicks were treated in exactly the same way and had the same chances of reaching adulthood. It can be seen from the information in Table 19 that the performance of the domestic birds was vastly superior in terms of the numbers of young produced. One of the reasons for failure of the 'wild' young was their susceptibility to the nestling diseases which are prevalent in captivity; few of them actually survived to the stage of fledging. The most likely explanation is that domestic birds have developed a high resistance to these diseases over the years in captivity, and their young are therefore sufficiently hardy to cope with most of the infections which are encountered in the nest. Wild birds have a low resistance to nestling diseases and often succumb to them.

Clearly, domestication of the Gouldian Finch is leading to change, and it will undoubtedly continue to do so, unless aviculturists decide to stop it. Some changes, such as resistance to disease, are certainly desirable, but others

TABLE 19
Various aspects of the breeding performance of wild-caught birds compared with that of domestic birds.

	Wild-caught birds	Domestic birds
Numbers of pairs	6	10
Numbers of pairs laying eggs	3	10
Mean number clutches per pair	2.3	6.0
Total number eggs	31	313
Mean number eggs per clutch	4.4	5.2
Total number eggs hatching	22	180
Per cent eggs hatching	71	58
Total numbers young fledging	5	165
Per cent young fledging	23	92

are more questionable. Aviculturists must decide whether they wish the Gouldian Finch to follow along the same lines as the budgerigar and canary, and change in qualities such as size, shape and colouration, or whether they would prefer it to remain very much the same bird as it is today. Whatever courses of action are decided, the control of its future as a cage bird must surely lie in the creation of, and adherence to, suitable breeding and show standards.

Many serious breeders eventually decide to put the results of their breeding efforts to the test by showing their birds. This is a highly specialist aspect of the hobby and one that is likely to require a lot of time and preparation in order to achieve good results. The Gouldian Finch performs well under 'show conditions' and satisfactory results can often be obtained without too much effort, but considerable commitment is needed to win consistently and to carry away the prizes at the most prestigious shows. There is also a conflict between the aims of showing and breeding. Showing, particularly transporting the birds to the show and the stress of the show itself, is bound to take something out of them, and is certainly not the ideal preparation for bringing birds into breeding condition. Some breeders prefer to show only their males since they come back into breeding condition more readily than females.

There are two basic types of show: the Members' Show at which entries are restricted to the members of the organising society; and the Open Show which is open to all-comers. There will be several separate classes, the precise number being governed largely by the anticipated size of the entry. Australian Finches are often allocated between one and five classes. There are commonly four which might, for example, be as follows.

I   Any variety of Gouldian Finch or Parrot Finch.
II   Longtail (including Hecks), Masked, and Parsons Finches.
III Any other species of Australian Finch.
IV   Any species (or variety) of Australian Finch which has been bred by the owner during the current year.

It is usually permissible to show birds either singly or in pairs.

PREPARING BIRDS FOR THE SHOW

It is usual practice to select the potential show team of birds as soon as they come through the moult, allowing maximum preparation time before the showing season starts. Selecting the best birds is always a problem but one way of doing this is to 'point' them against the standard described on pp. 116–117. The birds scoring the highest numbers of points are not only potentially good breeding stock but should also be good show birds. It is, in addition, necessary to check that members of the show team do not suffer from malformations, such as missing claws. Such deficiences may not be a breeding handicap but would lead to loss of points on the show bench.

Selected birds are caged separately in order to eliminate the risk of them causing feather damage to one another. The cages should be relatively small ones (e.g. $60 \times 30 \times 40$cm, $24 \times 12 \times 16$in) with two perches, which are positioned with one near the top and one near the floor of the cage in order to keep the birds fit (see Chapter 8). As the showing season nears, the perches are placed at the same level (about half-way up the cage) so that they become used to the configuration of show cages. The diet should be varied but not too rich (e.g. in soft food), otherwise the birds may become obese and lethargic.

Plumage condition is of paramount importance on the show bench and it can be improved by spraying during the preparation period. It should be started immediately the birds have settled into their new quarters, using a small plastic houseplant spray with an adjustable nozzle. Commercial plumage sprays are available but one can be made by dissolving one tablespoon (about 20ml) of glycerine in a cup of boiling water and then topping this up with cold, soft or boiled water. All food containers are removed from the cage before spraying starts and the cage is inspected to make sure that it is thoroughly clean, thereby avoiding the risk that the wet bird will soil its plumage. An easy way of doing this is to cover the floor each day with a fresh piece of absorbent paper. Spraying is best done in the middle of the day so that the birds are thoroughly dry before roosting time. They should be sprayed evenly over the whole body to the point of obvious wetness but should not be saturated. As the stock comes into showing condition, spraying is reduced to a fine mist, which is just sufficient to dampen the feathers. Two days before the show, it is stopped altogether, allowing the feathers to tighten up and the natural oils to build up, adding the extra sheen.

Show cage training starts early. Birds are enticed to enter the cages by hanging them on to the preparation cage fronts, and providing greenfood and other titbits in them. They soon learn that there is always something special inside the show cage and enter it readily. This method not only has the advantage of making the birds 'feel at home' in their show cages but it also ensures that they enter them without having to be caught, thereby preventing the high risk of damaged feathers. The birds spend the day before the show in their show cages.

SHOW CAGES

The cage shown in Fig. 25 is suitable for showing Gouldian Finches. It is of the desk front type and measures $39 \times 32 \times 19$cm ($15\frac{1}{2} \times 12\frac{1}{2} \times 7\frac{1}{3}$in). The spacing between the front wires is 1cm ($\frac{1}{2}$in) and the perches are 1cm ($\frac{1}{2}$in) in diameter and 14cm ($5\frac{1}{2}$in) long. The cages must be kept spotlessly clean. Their exteriors, including the wire fronts, are painted gloss black, and their interiors are painted with white vinyl silk emulsion. There is one water container attached to the interior of the bottom rail.

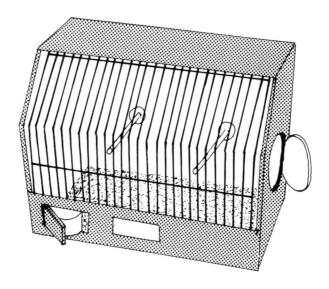

Fig. 25 *A show cage of the kind used to exhibit small finches.*

THE DAY OF THE SHOW

The birds are allowed at least one hour's light for feeding and drinking before they are transported to the show. Some people have special cases for packing and transporting show cages but others prefer to place a cloth cover over each show cage, protecting the birds in it from draughts and sudden frights. The water containers are emptied before transportation, to eliminate the risk of wet cages and bedraggled birds. It is also important to keep them at even temperatures during the journey. Extreme temperatures will neither help the birds nor do their chances on the show bench any good. Gouldian Finches are sometimes inclined to bathe in their water containers and thus it is advisable to leave these empty until after judging. However, care should be taken to ensure that stewards are briefed to fill them immediately afterwards so that the birds are not left without water.

The procedure on return from the show is important as the birds will have been subject to stress, despite the training, and should be treated accordingly. Keep them at about 30°C (85°F) and under constant light for the first day, and then watch them carefully for signs of distress, as conditions are gradually brought back to the normal ones.

WHAT ARE THE JUDGES LOOKING FOR?

General condition is of great importance. The judge will be looking for perfect, fully developed plumage. Damaged or missing feathers are faults, as are signs of an incomplete moult, however small they may be. Size, shape and colour are all essential qualities. A large bird is normally better than a small one, but only as long as it does not suffer from obvious defects, such as a dropped tail, pouted chest or crossed wings. Stance is also important; the bird must perch in a confident and proud manner, and must give every impression of being lively and active, without fluttering nervously around its cage.

Pairs must be chosen so that they complement one another, and must be of the same variety. Often one finds that pairs are unsuccessful because one of them is in imperfect show condition, whereas the non-offending partner would have been a sure winner if it had been shown on its own.

INDEX